How people have been helped by Tanenbaum's approach to the battle of the sexes:

Understands daughters better...

"Now that I know women are much more apt to think aloud than men and don't necessarily expect an immediate response or reaction, I understand my daughters better." **Steven B. Mason, Ph.D. Psychologist and Host, Radio Talk Show.**

Effective communication tools...

"Joe's ideas are provocative in the best possible way. They provoke us to re-examine old beliefs and emerge with new human understanding and more effective tools for communication." **Jerry Gillies, Best-selling author of** *Moneylove* **and** *Transcendental Sex.*

Better working relationships with men...

"This information has made a big difference in the way I approach communication with men in the workplace. Knowing how they think and view women, I have trained myself to be very focused. I set my agenda and stick to it. They listen to me, give me results and respect me. We know we are on the same side." **Leslie Dragon, Operations Manager, Lyncole Industries.**

"I learned to focus on the differences between men and women and their styles in the corporate world. Now I understand the ground rules men live by." **Kristine Robinson, Mgr., Equal Opportunity Programs, Douglas Aircraft Co.**

International business smoother...

"Conducting business on an international level can be particularly challenging with respect to communication. Using Joe's work allows me to find the common ground in all of us—regardless of our nationality." **Joseph M. Partise, International Insurance Consultant.**

Mother stops struggling with son...

"Before I had the material in this book it was not much fun and difficult for me to be with my son. Now we have a deep sense of connection and appreciation between us. I give him permission to be himself and experience him as if I was looking at him through his eyes. He feels loved and understood, and I gave up the struggle in our relationship." **Odilia McFarland, mother and bilingual language expert.**

School district spouses and colleagues see changed behavior...

"Mr. Tanenbaum's presentation to our school district's Administrators' Leadership Team received the highest rating of any human relations speaker to ever address our group. Co-workers and spouses who were not in attendance were fascinated by the heightened awareness of subtle behavior changes by those in attendance." **William R. Seaver, Superintendent of Schools, Canejo Valley Unified School District.**

Improved business and personal relationships...

"Understanding the differences in women and men and how to apply this in our everyday lives is timely information which is immediately applicable in building more effective corporate and personal relationships." **Robert Garland, Partner in Charge, Touche Ross & Company.**

"Applying these techniques to difficult business relationships changed them for the better almost immediately, and it was so simple." **Rosemary Maellaro, Behaviorial Specialist and past Human Resources Manager, The Southland Corporation.**

Understands women better...

"This book is the right tool at the right time! It has been an essential element to my successful interactions with my three daughters, a female business partner and increased numbers of women in key corporate positions. I can now exchange self-expression, understanding, and compassion at a level I did not previously suspect was there. Keep writing Joe!" **Richard Houser, Principal, Richard Houser Fine Art and Paragone Fine Art Gallery.**

Improved executive management skills...

"The techniques in this book work! Understanding the differences between men and women added a new dimension to my management and communication skills." **Josh Napua, Executive Vice President, Wyle Laboratories.**

"We are delighted to have Joe Tanenbaum and his interpersonal communication skills as a part of our executive training in the Lockheed Institute. Wish we had known about him a long time ago!" **Dr. Bill Henry, Ed. D., Director, Training & Development, Lockheed Corporation.**

MALE & FEMALE

REALITIES

Understanding The Opposite Sex

JOE TANENBAUM

CANDLE PUBLISHING COMPANY   **SUGAR LAND, TEXAS**

MALE & FEMALE REALITIES:
UNDERSTANDING THE OPPOSITE SEX

Published by:

Candle Publishing Company
101 Southwestern Blvd., Suite 210
Sugar Land, Texas 77478-3525

Library of Congress Cataloging-in-Publication Data

Tanenbaum, Joe, 1945-
   Male & female realities : understanding the opposite sex /
by Joe Tanenbaum
      p.cm.
   Bibliography: p.
   Includes index.
   ISBN 0-942523-36-9.   ISBN 0-942523-37-7 (pbk.)
   1. Sex differences (Psychology)   2. Sex differences.
   3. Interpersonal relations. I. Title
   BF692.2.T36   1989
   155.3'3—dc19
   88-38901

Compiled and documented from his case files during twenty-three years of corporate management experience, Male and Female Realities: Understanding the Opposite Sex, is the newest, biggest bridge across the Battleground of the Sexes into the relatively unexplored territory of personal identity.

His clients refer to his theories as Tanenbaum Timebombs - "tidbits of dynamite information that go off at just the right time!" You'll find out why when he takes you on an amazing exploration of the differences in male and female approaches to communication, sex, emotions, decisions, priorities, commitment, learning, and much more.

Mr. Tanenbaum is an interpersonal communication specialist, consultant, corporate trainer, speaker, workshop leader, and author. He founded Tanenbaum Associates to assist individuals, as well as Fortune 500 companies such as Delta Airlines, McDonnell Douglas, and Southland Corporation, in rebuilding and recovering compassion, trust, and esteem in interpersonal relationships. He has presented more than 600 workshops, led more than 30,000 man-hours of training, and appeared on numerous television and radio programs throughout the country.

Joe Tanenbaum's "truce or consequences" approach to the Battle of the Sexes is provocative in theory, practical in application, and universal in scope.

Also by Joe Tanenbaum

published by Candle Publishing Company:

A Man in the Mood:
Poems for Laughing, Loving, and Living

Audio Tapes

Men's & Women's Realities:
More Different Than You Think
6-Tape Album

Down to Earth:
Six Practical Talks on Interpersonal Relationships
6-Tape Album

Compassion
2-Tape Album

CONTENTS

ILLUSTRATIONS

DEDICATION

This book is dedicated to realizing the potential for peace and harmony on the planet. I strongly believe that we cannot achieve lasting satisfaction in our own lives until we all learn to live together in respect and love for life, have appreciation for the various ways life expresses itself, and develop compassion when life becomes the struggle that it sometimes can be. I dedicate this book to my mother, whose early training began these lessons for me to learn.

ACKNOWLEDGMENTS

The acknowledgments page has been the most difficult page in this book for me to write. There are so many people who have come in and out of my life during the last ten years while I was developing this material, giving lectures, and leading workshops, I was concerned that I would accidentally leave out a very special person. If I have done so, please call me. As a friend, you are probably already too aware of my faulty memory.

I would first like to acknowledge Richard Houser, whose personal and professional support has seen me through the best of times, and especially when I needed it the most, through the worst of times. And to all of the following, I extend my deepest appreciation:

To Leslie Dragon and Susan Kawakami Brietkopf whose friendships were severely tested in managing my office with limited resources and little direction while organizing material and typing transcripts.

To Kristine Kister Robinson for introducing and supporting my work in the corporate world.

To Stanlee Phelps, Pat Raffee, and Georgia Nobel for their feedback on the first draft.

To Carolyn Williams-McKim and Ed McKim for providing a sense of family, a place to live, and office space when I couldn't afford either.

To Keven Howe for our sushi, sake, and Rambo nights when I needed them most.

To Odilia McFarland for promoting my work and keeping it alive in the San Francisco area.

To Richard Winn for his special intelligence, humor, and work on the reference material.

To Warren Lyons and Judy Seigfried, just because.

To Josh and Pat Napua for Tahoe and much more.

To Lynne Sims for her vision as a publisher to make this book possible and for her friendship and generosity when both were needed.

To Carol Estes for her patience, love and dedication in pulling all the pieces of this book project together.

And especially to Jan Tanenbaum (formerly Jan Wienecke), my wife and the love of my life, for showing up just in the nick of time and for being an extremely talented and dedicated business partner.

FOREWORD

There are many articles and other publications which tell us about the biological differences between males and females, but none of them tell us how these differences impact our relationships—until now.

For the past ten years, I've studied Joe Tanenbaum's material about male and female realities and applied his information in my life at work and at home; with my children, my employees, and my peers.

I was skeptical when I first heard Joe's theories because I thought I knew as much as I needed to know about the sexes. After all, I had been married 22 years, reared a son and daughter, and had worked in a man's world since age 16. But then I began to pay closer attention to male and female behavior, my own included. Through this gradual process of observation, objectivity, and open-mindedness, I began to realize how much I didn't know. I also realized how much I had distorted my own female energy in order to survive; and was totally ignorant of the male energy I possessed, even though it could have helped me in so many situations and circumstances.

Most people would agree that the idea of peace in the world will manifest when we express peace in our daily lives. The Battle of the Sexes, however, has been quietly waged for centuries. It has cost all of us a tremendous price, though we may not realize it. Whether ignorance of our differences manifests as broken hearts or missed sales, we chip away at our own and others' self-esteem each time we "fail" in relationship with another. Knowing how our biological differences affect our behavior gives us the opportunity to make wiser choices about our daily lives and allows us to interact with other members of the human family with greater compassion. It is the most practical and powerful knowledge I've received in all my learning years as a corporate executive, a wife, and a mother.

What's really exciting to me is that Mr. Tanenbaum's information is not "cut and dried" nor formal nor final—he has just opened the biggest, newest bridge for exploring the realms of male and female identity.

Now the questions and the real fun begins. At least they have for me: How do I get myself into healthy balance? How can I help others meet their male and female gender needs? How can the male and female needs of a business or institution be met and still affect the bottom line in a positive manner? What are the male and female needs of our wonderful planet and how can I help ensure that these needs are met for future generations?

We truly have an opportunity in our relationships to experience ecstacy or extinction. This applies to us as a species as well. How much greater capacity we will have to bring happiness, peace, and prosperity to our world when we not only recognize but honor our differences.

Lynne Sims

Publisher and Author

REALITIES

INTRODUCTION

Have you often felt that no matter how you alter or rearrange yourself, you don't seem able to make your interactions with the opposite sex smoother? Do you perceive yourself as just too emotional, or them as too unemotional? Are you too organized, or are they always in a state of confusion? Are you really too flighty, or are they too serious? At home or at work, how does it happen that unquestionable facts from your "reality" become so misunderstood or misinterpreted by someone else?

How we perceive reality (our own and the reality of others) is filtered through the physical organism known as our body, and of course the body has a mind. How this organism functions is very important in understanding our reactions to "reality." The male body and mind differs greatly from the female body and mind, yet our tendency as human beings is to ignore these important differences and interpret reality according to our own gender signals. Most men's internal signals—interpreting aggression or friendship, for example—have evolved so that men can appropriately interact with other men. Likewise, women's internal signals have evolved so that women can interact with other women. When another person's behavior doesn't fit within the realm of our own familiar gender signals, we get

1

confused. Worse, we harbor unrealistic expectations that are bound to be disappointed, or we make assumptions that aren't justified.

The thousands of people who have participated in my Men's and Women's Reality Workshops over the past ten years have come from very different cultural, racial, social, and economic backgrounds. I have presented this information to members of corporations and religious organizations, at high schools and colleges, to medical and mental health professionals, and to people visiting from other countries—a virtual potpourri of humanity. And what quickly becomes apparent in virtually every setting is that men and women have difficulty truly appreciating each other. My women clients are certain that men are indulging in exasperating "male" behavior, while men are equally certain that women are indulging in exasperating "female" behavior. Women think that men would be perfect if only they weren't "broken" and need to be fixed; men feel exactly the same way about women, and each sex feels demeaned by this perception in the other.

You and I have heard hundreds of jokes about men, women, relationships, and marriage. Some of the jokes are funny and make us laugh at our circumstances, but unfortunately, jokes usually hide anger, misunderstandings, and fears.

One thing is clear, and it is that both men and women are waiting for the other sex to change their behavior. Fortunately, we have not been able to "fix" each other, even though we've been trying for thousands of years! Consider: to a woman, a "fixed man" would be almost indistinguishable from another woman, and a man would find that a "fixed woman" would act like "one of the boys" all the time! Talk about mass confusion! It might even be worse than it is now!

Despite all the real enlightenment achieved over the last couple of decades, the "battle of the sexes" exists and continues to escalate because of limited understanding of the "enemy." You may believe that you understand what is being said to you by a member of the opposite sex because men and women use the same basic language (English, in our case). But we assume that a word (or the personal experience relating to a word) is the same for everyone, even though we know that the meaning of a word may change by region of country, by race or religion, and certainly between generations. What we usually overlook is how words are interpreted differently because of gender.

In addition to the possibility of a language barrier between males and females, we shall see that each gender has different internal signals that define positive and negative feedback. Some of these signals are inborn and others are learned in order to survive in our respective environments, but we continue to experience and act on these signals, even though survival may no longer be an issue.

In exploring these issues, it is not my intention to support ignorant or suppressive male or female chauvinistic attitudes. However, some attitudes have a seed of truth to them, and it is important to investigate that seed for the source of the behavior or the misinterpretation of that behavior.

A typical example of seemingly harmless misinterpretation came from a couple who participated in one of my workshops. We were discussing the appreciation that most women have for flowers. As a token of his love for her, this particular man had bought his wife a beautiful long-stemmed rose. She was thrilled with his spontaneity, romanticism, and thoughtfulness. He was so pleased that his love token was appreciated that the following week he went out and bought her another long-stemmed rose. She enjoyed it, but was a bit less thrilled the second time and showed slightly less appreciation for his gesture. By the third week, and after his third consecutive long-stemmed rose, she simply smiled and said, "Thank you." He was quite confused by her declining enthusiasm, but he was persistent. He knew he had the right idea, but he wasn't quite sure what to change for her in order to recapture her initial enthusiasm and appreciation. So the next week he bought her a crystal rose. She was thrilled. It had worked! So the following week, he bought her another crystal rose. You know the rest of the story.

Insensitive and inconsiderate behavior appears in both men and women. But considerate behavior can often be misconstrued as inconsiderate behavior if it is not what is expected. In the man's attempt to please the woman, he looked for something he could do that would let her know how much he loved her. He was not being lazy by getting her the same thing week after week. He simply wanted something that would consistently communicate his love. (I will explain why men like consistency in Chapter 8.) It worked the first time, therefore he believed it should always work. Once you have found something a man enjoys, you can almost guarantee that he will always be pleased with it. Men seem to have an underlying rule, "If it's not broken, don't fix it!" Therefore, in the case of the long-stemmed rose, the woman appeared to be fickle, unappreciative, and unable or unwilling to be pleased. To the woman, the man appeared unimaginative, lazy, and redundant. Neither assumption was true, but the misinterpretation had taken its toll on the relationship.

After reading this book you will probably ask more questions of the opposite sex rather than assume you understand what is being said. I predict that you will also begin to trust what is being said by listening to and being willing to understand the differences in male and female experiences. And I guarantee you will find yourself in a number of situations that you will be able to resolve easily, and that many of these situations would have presented themselves as problems before you read this book.

Sex-based differences affect our business lives as well as our personal relationships. In the chapters that follow, you will learn how these differences determine management styles, corporate structure, and leadership choices, as well as roles within the family. You may also begin to develop more compassion and trust for yourself and others as you begin to understand the different motivations and realities of men and women. You will also learn to discern different styles of men and women which will allow you to discover and accept your own unique style.

Once you have discovered your own truth (as opposed to what you think should be true about your personality because of others' opinions or instructions), you may find that your gender identification shifts many times. You may identify with both "male" and "female" attributes, or you may identify with just one model. As you develop a greater sense of what is "normal" behavior for you, you may no longer be willing to put up with behavior (in yourself or those around you) that is demeaning or insensitive to your needs.

For me, the complexity of human options is the joy of living together on this planet. The wonder and variety of life, the discovery of our differences, and the celebration of our uniqueness allow us to see the individual contribution we make to the tapestry of human existence. It is with this thought in my heart that I pursue our "differences."

1

WHY MALES AND FEMALES WANT TO KNOW MORE ABOUT EACH OTHER

Over the years, I have examined the behavior of men and women from an unusual premise—a premise that has proven to open doors of communication and understanding for thousands of men and women in all types of relationships. My premise is simple:

◊ All humans are created equal but not created the same.
◊ Humans have confused the notions of "same" and "equal."
◊ The ways in which men and women have evolved cause different behavior and different perceptions.
◊ Neither "male" or "female" behavior is "wrong."

This book is written to explain why we behave as we do. I intend to give you practical information that will be immediately useful to you in your personal and professional life.

Once presented with this information, the participants in my Men's and Women's Reality Workshops have said:

◊ "I thought there was something wrong with me for not wanting to do it his (or her) way."
◊ "I thought that was something unique to my husband (or wife). He told me what he was thinking or feeling, but I couldn't relate.

5

I thought he was lying to me, or at least holding back the real truth.''

◇ "I was shocked to see how I have discounted my wife's (husband's) feelings because I thought she was indulging herself. I always wondered why she couldn't be more like me. Now I know, and I have apologized to her!''

Once in a while, I like to traipse through history and see how much the human species has changed. Not long ago, I browsed through a book of quotations from the previous 2,000–5,000 years. Later, in a workshop, I read some of these quotes in a seminar and asked the participants, "When do you think these were written?''

Their answers varied slightly, but most said, "Oh, that's obviously from the sixties,'' or "That's from the seventies,'' or "That's from the forties.'' And my point was made, for every one of the quotations I had read to them about men, women, and relationships was at least 3,000 years old!

I suggest that the environment or context we live in shapes the words we use and some of our basic forms of expression (style of dress, manners, customs, and the like), but that the foundation of our relationships is controlled by our evolution as a species.

One commonly held theory suggests that when the human brain was evolving, males and females were performing different ecological functions. Females gathered food and nurtured babies; males hunted. Since these activities required different skills, adaptive pressures influenced brain development. Females, for example, needed a more integrated understanding of the world (holistic, community based), while males required more specialized skills, such as the ability to hold three-dimensional images in the mind. A man's survival depended on how he got along with other men in the world—not how he got along with women.

Male and female issues today are essentially the same issues men and women dealt with 100,000 years ago. Back then, however, the issue was survival of the species; survival of self came second. These early survival issues not only limited opportunities, but also kept our ancestors from having to look at the chronic underlying rifts between men and women. After all, it has only been within the last 150 years or so that men and women have had to start "talking" to each other. Since life was about surviving and raising the family, there was not a lot of reason or even social time for such questions as, "What are you doing this weekend?" It's only recently that we've begun to ask, "Would you like to sit and talk?"—only to discover that we can't. Until now, it hasn't been necessary. But today males and females have to develop an ability to communicate.

WHAT'S THE PROBLEM, ANYWAY?

I always ask people what they want to get out of my workshops, and these comments are fairly representative:

Robert: "...to revive some thoughts and ideas on bettering my current relationship, as well as my relationships with women on the job."

Bill: "I want to sharpen the ability to act and react to get what I want and to gain more personal freedom. Also, to make my wife feel that same freedom and be able to relax with me."

Charley: "...a better understanding of who I am as a member of the male species...."

Ken: "...insight on male/female relationships and...how to control some of my feelings toward women."

Mark: "...to have a better understanding of women and how to communicate...to develop a better relationship with my wife of sixteen years."

Carl: "...how to deal with people of the opposite sex to understand their needs, their wants, and some of the problems they have been incurring in the work force."

Fred: "...to improve my relationship with my wife—understand her temper tantrums and why she does what she does."

Larry: "I'm here for myself—the relationship with myself."

Rick: "...for putting greater fun and lightheartedness into all of my relationships."

Paul: "...for the building and dismantling of appropriate or inappropriate walls."

Kyle: "...to learn to be less tolerant of behavior that does not support my well-being. I find myself saying, 'It's okay, it doesn't matter,' when it really does!"

Jessica: "I want to be able to relate to men better and not to be as threatened by them and their behavior."

Carol: "I happen to like men. I really don't want to change them, but I would like to know them better or understand them better."

Rhonda: "I would like to have a better understanding of women...because I find that I am really critical of women and the way that they operate in business."

Debra: "I would like to understand men better in a business context so that I can compete better with them. I would like to have more empathy for women in my life—those who work in my home, those who are my clients, those who are my employees in the office...."

Carrie: "I would like to relate better with myself and other women."

Georgia: "I haven't had a real relationship for the past three years. So I'm kind of wondering what's causing that, or what's hindering me."

Lori: "I find that...the male role and the female role are getting very muddled in our society right now...."

Ella: "I need to know what is important to the opposite sex so that I don't make them feel uncomfortable and not willing to be vulnerable so that I can really get to know who they are."

Lois: "...my wish would be to be a man for a day. I think that if I could walk in a man's shoes, I would probably be much more compassionate and maybe adore them too."

Tricia: "It gets kind of confusing always having to change behavior if you're with women or when you're with men."

Susanne: "I'm a pretty strong person, but I lost my identity. I think a lot of it was because I was programmed to submit—we had children and that was it."

It seems obvious from the above comments that men and women are pursuing the same results: They want to fix the problems that exist between genders. Yet male and female assumptions about *how* to fix the problems are so different that we've begun to think of each other as enemies on the same destructive path.

There are many philosophies about how creation occurred and how we came to be human beings. Evolution and socialization have modified our biology somewhat in order to take advantage of greater opportunities as a species. But once we're in a body, each body expresses itself differently. As a male or female, we have a "range" of behavior, and, granted, socialization determines what we do with that range, but the range is predetermined by our biological vehicle. I'm not saying what men or women can or can't do, because the mind can make modifications to many functions in the body. I'm suggesting what is *natural* for males and females. We can "put up" with a lot of things from, or because of, the opposite sex and give up part of ourselves in the process, but too often we do so blindly, without being aware of the alternatives.

If you were raised in a gender-dominant household (that is, with a very strong father or mother, or with several siblings of the opposite sex), you may have had to suppress yourself in order to get along. You probably became accustomed to being misunderstood, or you got used to the emptiness, or you accepted not being able to express yourself as needed. After a while, you forgot your needs. Now, you may find yourself trying to adjust to being "out of balance," and you don't know why.

Love becomes sacrifice when you suppress yourself enough that you forget who you are in the relationship. And once you demean yourself to prove that you love somebody, your anger gets directed at that person for "putting you" in that position, or you hate yourself for having "submitted."

When you discover what is healthy for you, you will become less tolerant of others' opinions of what you should be doing with your life. You will begin to realize that *you* are the most knowledgeable person about you and your well-being. Then, when someone recommends that you change something about yourself, you will have the option of openly considering the advice and following it or not, depending on your sense of what is appropriate for you—not because you think you "should."

You may have certain gifts that actually appear threatening to the opposite sex. You may have stopped displaying or utilizing these gifts, or you may have forgotten that you ever had them. One of the best examples of a "lost gift" is a story that was told in a women-only workshop I was leading. One woman told the group, "You know how there are times when you're going to the airport and you're late and there's no possible way you can make the plane on time? You have ten miles left to go, but in an instant you discover you're five miles closer. Five miles of the highway has just disappeared! It's gone." (Many of the women in the room knew exactly what this woman was talking about.)

Men and male-trained women would explain this phenomenal gift as "You somehow became unconscious," or "You misread your clock," or "You *thought* it was ten miles, but it was only five." No wonder women have trained themselves not to say those kinds of things! If they do, they will not be taken seriously. Men (and male-trained women) will say, "You can't trust her." As a metaphor for the differences we'll be exploring, I suggest that every woman can and does alter time. During workshop lunch break, I asked the women who said they could alter time to sit with the women who said they couldn't. Within a few hours the women who said they couldn't, began to remember how to recover that ability—some women within minutes!

Imagine a woman in a car with a man, and she says, "Oh, don't worry, we'll make it. I'll just disappear five miles of this highway. " The man will either assume he is riding with a "flake" or tell her, "You can't do that." Women have hidden this ability, just to avoid a fight (which seems like an innocent concession at the time), or they will suppress themselves without knowing why. The point is that men distrust feminine behavior and abilities they don't understand, and women distrust male behavior and abilities they don't understand.

Most of the time we don't believe what the other gender is saying because it is so alien to our reality that we can't imagine the other person is telling the truth. If a woman asks a man, what do you need? he's usually capable of furnishing a list of exactly what he needs. The items on his list that fit her own reality may be okay, but she may interpret some of his other needs as disgusting, annoying, stupid, inconsiderate, or unbelievably selfish.

We are aware of the wide range of styles, personalities, biology, and chemistry that makes each of us uniquely different. I suggest, though, that the differences between men and women are much greater than the individual differences between two people of the same gender.

STYLE DIFFERENCES

Even within genders, there is a wide variety of styles: what makes us happy, how we respond to difficulty, how we express ourselves, what kind of jobs we like. I also suggest that the most feminine man is more male than the most masculine woman. For example, a gay man who attended one of my workshops was very upset with me but didn't let me know until months later. Then he approached me and said:

"You know, I was really annoyed with you and didn't even want to talk to you after going through the workshop. I was listening to everything you were saying, and it all applied to the other men in the room, but it really didn't apply to me. Everything you said about women, I could relate to, and all the stuff you said about men, I couldn't. So I went back to my girlfriends [he had a group of women as friends], and we had a conversation about the cute guys we were dating. It was a lot of fun. All of a sudden, I had to prove that you were wrong about me and how it is for me, so in the middle of the conversation, I said to them, 'I know what you mean. You mean so-and-so.' All the women turned to me and said, 'No, that's not what we're talking about.' I said, 'Oh, I know what you mean,' and I tried again. Since they were using the same English, and we were all talking about the same subject, I assumed that their experience and their expression of their experience was the same. And it wasn't! All that time, I thought we had so many things in common, and we really didn't. In addition to not having male friends, I felt like I was losing my female friends.

One of the reasons I took the workshop was to learn how to have men friends who weren't lovers. I wanted to be able to have a man-to-man relationship. So I went through that stage. Then I realized why I didn't have any male friends, why I didn't have that comradery, why I wasn't able to relate to men. It was because I thought the things in me that were masculine denied my being gay and had to be suppressed. I had held back because I couldn't conceive of being that masculine and being gay and still enjoying myself. I had suppressed that within me, which kept the other men around me from being able to relate man-to-man. After that realization, I was able to acquire male friends; I was able to go back to the women and enjoy sharing things with them. Now I have it all. So even though I was angry with you at the start, I want to thank you for giving me more balance in my life.''

My goal here is not just about how you can relate more realistically to yourself, but also how you can develop more tolerance for other styles of men and women. Some members of your own gender may cause you to say, ''I'm embarrassed to have men [or women] like that around.'' Your embarrassment may actually stem from the recognition that you have some of the same tendencies, characteristics, or desires, only you have suppressed them, or they have been trained out of you. By deepening your perceptions, you can start to look at others and say, ''Oh, there's a piece of me; I can relate to that,'' as opposed to judging the other person and separating yourself from him or her.

THE MYTH OF "REALITY"

Much of what is called ''reality'' has to do with male reality (as opposed to ''the'' reality). Some of the intolerance that women talk about is directly related to this slanted perception of how things should be. Both genders have a natural ''framework'' which is healthy for them, but it may be damaging for the opposite sex. What needs to be healed are our relationships with other men or women, as well as those parts of us that are suppressed, analyzed, or manipulated.

To begin this enterprise, we should be aware of how uneasy we often feel about being identified with our own genders. If I attributed to a woman some of the male characteristics her gender sometimes displays, she would probably be annoyed. For example, if I said, ''You're analytical, you're focused, you're inflexible, you're not communicative enough, and you have no compassion,'' she might be highly insulted. Yet if I said to another man, ''You're a gorilla,'' the man would probably say, ''Thank you. I've always felt like one.'' On the other hand, if I said to a woman, ''You're acting just like a woman,'' it also has a negative connotation. It is sad that most of us can be so easily insulted by being included in our own gender category. ''Yes, thank you, I am a man [or woman],'' is a response I suggest we can all practice.

There are certain qualities that men have in common, ways of behaving that women find annoying or childish. It's possible that this is just the way some men are, and women take it personally as if men are deliberately acting that way. There are also certain things that women have in common, yet men tend to deny or deride this commonality because it may not be comfortable or appropriate in their male reality.

My observations have led me to the opinion that men and women are not designed to be around each other all the time; we're not designed to balance one-on-one. Many relationships die from suffocation. If one of the individuals (rarely is it both) wants to be around the other partner constantly, it's usually an unhealthy sign. Although there are times for us to be with the opposite sex, there are times when it is appropriate for men to be with men and women to be with women. Men and women have lost that time when they can just relax and not worry about what is said, their manners, or being "socialized." In the next chapter, we'll see how we persist in thinking of our differences as negative, when they are actually only differences.

CHAPTER SUMMARY:

The environment or context we live in shapes the words we use and our basic forms of expression.

Adaptive pressures influenced brain development as we evolved.

Male and female relationship issues today are basically the same issues men and women dealt with 100,000 years ago.

Males and females have to develop an ability to communicate; until now, it hasn't been necessary.

Men and women are seeking solutions to gender issues.

Males and females have a "range" of behavior.

Our range of behavior is predetermined to a great extent by our biologically inherited characteristics.

Automatic responses are different in men and women because of body chemistry and brain organization.

Behavior, which includes automatic responses, allows us to identify gender.

A man's survival was dependent on how he got along with other men
    in the world.

We assume behavior unlike our own is inappropriate and needs to be
    fixed.

You are the most knowledgable person about yourself and your
    well-being.

You may have certain "gifts" that actually appear threatening to the
    opposite sex.

Even within genders, there is a wide variety of "styles."

Our own assumptions get in the way of "reality."

Men and women are not designed to be around each other all the time.

2

WHAT MALES AND FEMALES WOULD "FIX" ABOUT THE OTHER

One of the questions I usually ask in my workshops is, "What would you fix or change about the opposite sex?" I have found that basically all women's responses are almost identical, regardless of the social, economic, religious, or cultural mix of the group (including teenagers to retirees); and the men's responses are also alike. My question deliberately emphasizes the awareness that men and women perceive our differences as negative rather than simply as "differences." Here are some of the responses.

MEN ON WOMEN

Male participant: "They're sissies. They're weak. If there is a jar to be opened, they come over: 'Can you open this?' and you know very well they can open it."

Male participant: "They are emotional. They're never logical. I hate that. They hate sports. Do you know a woman who will accept a man watching a basketball game? They cannot understand it."

Male participant: "When women grow older, they're just too serious, and they can't understand why guys just like to go out and have fun."

Male participant: "They have less sexual desire. They can't take a punch. Disorganized. Moody. Negative. Vengeful. And late."

Male participant: "They talk too much, and about the stupidest things. They change their minds constantly. They won't take control when you offer them control. They are vain. They nag. They pout."

Male participant: "They want to be mother forever. And that goes for mom, girlfriend, anything."

Male participant: "Too emotional, flippant, whimsical, capricious. They over-react. They have this typical knee-jerk reaction. They change their minds too quickly. Sometimes they are too sensitive—it's like you're walking on eggshells versus being able to 'roll with the punches.'"

Male participant: "They like you to read their minds."

Male participant: "They [women] want everything. They're parasitic in nature, and overly possessive of children."

Male participant: "They use sex to control you."

Male participant: "They find the perfect man and then spend the rest of their life fixing him."

Male participant: "They want the flowers, but they're unwilling to shovel the manure. They can pick up an axe and kill an alligator if they have to, but in daily transactions they use this delicate business."

WOMEN ON MEN

Female participant: "They always feel like they do everything better. Even though I know what I'm talking about, they don't listen to me. They always expect me to be perfect, even though they're not. They are very demanding; they put their values on me."

Female participant: "Always looking for a way to get me in bed. Not really affectionate. Very self-absorbed."

Female participant: "I find men always calling for accountability from me. I find that I have a tendency to bring out hostility in men; I threaten them terribly, and I find them defensive with me. And because they are defensive, they then become antagonistic."

Female participant: "Not spontaneous. Sloppy. Unattentive. Not too creative. Judging. Evaluative. Take things for granted."

Female participant: "Expect me to put their needs and problems first. Always think that their job is more important than mine. Often tell me that I don't understand, don't know the facts, or am not acquainted with the reality of the situation. And they keep score—sometimes over years."

Female participant: "They are non-verbal. Often you want to have a conversation with them and you get grunts. They are often emotionally stunted. They lack intuition. They are too focused. If a guy is driving the car, it's like 'turn off the radio and shut up; I've got to make a left-hand turn.' They aren't able to do more than one thing at a time."

Female participant: "There's a strange way that they click in and out of crudity and insensitivity. And even though they allow themselves the expression and spontaneity, they don't want a woman to act the same way."

Female participant: "I usually take care of the really sticky problems on a one-to-one basis. He takes care of the finances. But if there is a human problem, I'm the one who has to do that."

Female participant: "Not intuitive. Uncompassionate. Don't like shopping."

Female participant: "Don't want to talk about their emotions."

Female participant: "Expect me to keep track of where he puts and loses things."

Female participant: "I would like men to share more in household chores, be a partner with me, and not make me feel like an employee."

It's easy to see in The Fix'em List how the summarized responses line up: literally men on one side and women on the other—in battle formation—with opposite "shoulds" for ammunition!

The Fix'em List

Men fixing women	Women fixing men
Women "should":	*Men "should":*
Talk less	Talk more
Be less emotional	Be more emotional
Be more physical	Be less physical
Be less "romantic"	Be more "romantic"
Want more sex	Want less sex
Be less involved with others' problems	Care more about people
Laugh less	Lighten up. Be silly
Be more rational	Be more spontaneous
Be more serious	Have more fun
Put job/career first	Put family first
Stay home more	Go out of the home more
Change less	Be more flexible
Have less attention on clothes	Have more attention on how they dress
Spend less time getting ready	Have more attention on personal hygiene
Be less sensitive	Be more compassionate
Be on time	Be more flexible with time

Each gender believes that what they are saying is *true*, that these are "facts," not opinions. There is agreement among men and women about these "facts." For example, men repeatedly comment in my workshops about women playing the "I'm too sensitive game."

Is she "acting more sensitive" or is she actually more sensitive? The *fact* is, women *are* more sensitive than men in a number of ways. (Chapter 5, "How the Biological Differences Affect Behavior," gives details of our differences.) What looks like indulgence on a woman's part may actually be a limitation imposed on her by her physical structure, just as there are some physical things about a man that a woman finds annoying or disgusting or rude:

"Why didn't you shave tonight?"

"Well, if you had to shave your face every day, you would know why sometimes I don't."

The men's list accuses women of being overly sensitive. The women's list says the men are insensitive. Every one of the items on the men's list is exactly the opposite of those on the women's. Women are saying, "If only you were more like me, then you would be okay." And men are saying, "If only you were more like me, then we could relate." Those behaviors we try to change in each other are based on the assumption that each gender is indulging in inappropriate behavior. Yet both men and women assume that we're all on the same side, seeing the same reality.

A woman in one of my workshops gave a perfect example. She was talking about being with her "idiot" husband in the car. (At the beginning of their relationship, everything was wonderful, of course, and he was Prince Charming!):

"You would think that after nine years, this idiot would know that when we're driving together, I like to take off my shoes, loosen my clothing, relax, and enjoy the ride. When we park, I've got to put on my shoes, tighten my clothing, and get out of the car. After nine years, he should expect that. Instead, he still gets upset when we arrive someplace and he wants to go right in, but I'm sitting there getting ready. You would think this guy would wake up to this one day!"

When we look at this situation from his point of view, we realize he assumes that after nine years of riding with him, she knows that he likes to get out of the car as soon as they park. That's important to him. Why sit there and waste time? Yet there she is, fixing her shoes. He calculates that it takes twelve seconds to put on shoes, twenty-three seconds to straighten hose, nineteen seconds.... Okay, so it looks like she needs three-and-a-half minutes to re-dress. To him, she should start to re-dress three-and-a-half minutes before they arrive at their destination. Then, the moment he parks the car, she should be ready to get out. Makes sense to him! He can only assume his passenger is an idiot—no question about it! And both of them are waiting for the other to change.

SAME VERSUS EQUAL

Men and women constantly confuse "equal" and "same." Women assume that being treated as an equal means that men should treat them like another woman would treat them. When men do treat women as equals, then women are insulted, because they don't want to be treated the way the man would treat another man. "You want to be treated like an equal? Then be willing to take a punch." Male buddies are always having contests. Everything can be tested in fun.

Men say, "Let's measure something. I don't care what it is."

Women say, "Well, that's not fun for me."

The man says, "But that's what I do for fun. I thought you wanted to be an equal here."

Both genders become confused because it appears that we lie to one another when we say one thing and mean something else. This might explain how and why men get confused in the job market when women say, "I want to be treated as an equal."

On the other hand, men wouldn't like to be treated as women. As one male participant argued, "We're not going around asking to be treated equal, to be treated like women!"

My observation has been that in a lot of ways, men *are* seeking the same kind of compassion and sensitivity that women are. Men want to be able to do things with women that they do with their male friends. Men want to relax and lighten up and have some fun too. But the male definition of lightening up, relaxing, and having fun is totally different than a female's. The words may be the same, but the meanings are very different. Men say they want some compassion in a sensual relationship. (Women mean romance; men mean sex.) There's a very different motivation which results in a totally different experience. It might be easier for men and women to communicate if we spoke different languages. Then at least we might ask, "What do you mean by that?" more often! Unfortunately, however, both genders mistakenly assume they know what the other is talking about. Let's begin learning how to put an end to the endless misunderstanding, and take a look at why these differences matter.

CHAPTER SUMMARY:

Men and women perceive gender differences as negative rather than simply as "differences."

Each gender perceives their negative opinion of the other as fact.

Every item on the men's Fix'em List is exactly opposite of the women's list for men.

Men and women confuse "equal" and "same."

It appears that we lie to one another when we say one thing and mean something else.

Men are seeking compassion and sensitivity.

Both genders mistakenly assume that we speak the same language, but the experience behind the word is different.

3

WHY THE DIFFERENCES COUNT

Men and women are very different biologically, and the differences are not limited to our reproductive organs. If we disregard style of dress, length of hair, jewelry, facial hair, exterior expressions, and the dictates of society and culture, we would still be able to distinguish between a man and a woman. A more extensive listing of the differences appears in Chapter 5; here we shall briefly ponder on the consequences.

In measuring the biological differences, one study I heard about determined that the human male has more in common with some other species, particularly apes, than with human females. Whether a fictitious study or not, this comparison will not be news to most women.

Many of us are working to establish and maintain equality between women and men. This equality will be realized and sustained through a growing awareness of our individual needs, compassion for our differences, and sensitivity to our individual rights. Meanwhile, however, in our attempt to eliminate inappropriate discrimination, we sometimes overlook the effects of enforced equality where real—not chauvinistic or racist—*unchangeable* differences exist. This book is written to shed light on that male and female behavior as it *appears,* not to determine if the behavior is appropriate. If we can demystify and accept the differences between us, we can move beyond pointing out the problems and get on to open communication.

SCAPEGOATS ARE PLENTIFUL

Attitudes and emotions can be convenient scapegoats for explaining behavior that is otherwise unexplainable. **The physically predetermined differences between male and female behavior have not been identified in their proper context, and I suggest that herein lies the solution to most of our relationship "problems."**

Differences in our muscle and skeletal structure, brain size and brain chemistry, the size and placement of our internal organs, hormones and endorphins of various unpredictable quantities, metabolic rates, breathing rates, eyesight, skin sensitivity, glands, and all other biological functions translate into different perceptions of situations and different approaches to solutions.

Breaking free of stereotypical identification is an important goal; surely discouraging or otherwise preventing an individual from attempting a task (or suggesting that he or she is incapable) when that person is perfectly capable of accomplishing the desired result is suppressive and manipulative. Equally significant, however, but almost always overlooked, is expecting an individual to do something which is not within their natural capacity. For example, if I have musical ability and I am stopped from pursuing that expression of myself, I will be suppressed and frustrated. On the other hand, if I am born into a family of musically talented people but I am tone-deaf, or have no aptitude for rhythm, I may be teased or even punished into practicing harder. Yet no matter how hard I practice, I will never be able to compete or participate with my family at their level and will probably feel "inferior." Nevertheless, I still have many options. I could be lovingly accepted by the family, even with my "limitation"; I could join a group of musicians who share my talent level; or I could become the family's manager and book their shows across the country.

We are all familiar with older children who take advantage of the undeveloped physical or intellectual abilities in younger children. Some adults maintain that type of childish behavior by treating each other as children who are not fully developed. We all have areas in our lives that continue to grow and develop, but as adults we need to yield to reality. And we need compassion for ourselves and others in order to look for the "gift" that may be hiding in a way of behaving that is perceived as a limitation.

Beyond the very obvious, there are thousands of physical differences between men and women. These differences cause men and women to have different points of view and very different approaches to situations. What the differences are, are much easier to discuss than what the differences mean. But it is illuminating to understand that gender modes and codes affect our attitudes, emotions, decisions, and solutions.

CHILDREN HAVE GENDERS TOO

It is very common for parents to overlook the effects of gender as it relates to children's behavior.

Many mothers hope that they will be able to keep their little boys from turning out to be stereotypical "men," and they sometimes have difficulty in finding common ground with their sons. It is fascinating and often disconcerting to see that boys show little or no interest in their mother's collection of dolls or in other memorabilia that she lovingly saved from her own childhood. Boys are interested in such fun games as belching contests (or contests related to any other part of the body that can be used to make funny and disgusting noises). Mothers soon discover that their sons like to watch games that result in people bleeding or bones breaking.

Knowing physical and emotional limits is very important to the male development. It is typical for brothers and buddies to form a bond in physical pain. (Girls form bonds through emotional pain.) Boys love to hurt each other. They also constantly invent situations that require leaping on each other from beds, dressers, tables, or stairways. When they engage in these sometimes exasperating activities, they are actually testing the tensile strength of their arms, legs, and ribs. Minor cuts, bruises, and nosebleeds often result, for boys test their limits of pain with almost any endurance contest imaginable. Eating, breathing, lifting, and swallowing contests are quite normal.

Boys' personal hygiene is another area of difference. Ask mothers about the shower. Just standing under the water might be perceived as concession enough, and very clever boys learn how to move the soap around in order to avoid suspicion (we shall be remarking later on the male sense of smell!). As a boy, I could blissfully spend an entire afternoon with my best friends throwing smelly, rolled-up socks into a wastebasket! A mother may discover that her son lost his toothbrush six months ago and didn't bother to tell her. (After all, if you tell her you lost it, she'll just get you another one.) Getting little boys to change their socks and underpants is a challenge, and boys never really learn the apparent joy of tissues. If women weren't around, boys wouldn't need tissues; they would use shirt sleeves, tablecloths, or a nasal blast to the ground.

Just as mothers need to expect such behavior on the part of their sons, so fathers need to be more tolerant with their daughters. Some girls enjoy rough and tumble play, and Daddy needs to be careful of overprotecting "his little angel." He also needs to be careful not to apply "boys rules" to her behavior—for example, training her not to pay attention to her emotional needs, telling her not to laugh so much, cautioning her to be more serious because he translates her joy as a lack of attention or commitment. A father's confusion about women in general is often translated through his behavior with his daughter; if he treats her without regard to sex, his tendency will be to make her a buddy, someone to teach and train to be like him. Many fathers teach their daughters how to please a man without realizing that they are training her to ignore some of her needs.

ARE YOU MALE-TRAINED OR FEMALE-TRAINED?

Usually after my lectures, at least one person will approach me and say, "Everything you said about the opposite sex seems to apply to me. Why are you describing me as if I were the opposite sex?"

To further complicate male/female modes and codes, our early upbringing greatly influences the expression of our behavior as adults. Not only is each individual a male or a female with varying proportions of both male and female energy, but we have been male-trained or female-trained, depending on our early environment. Most of us are sufficiently confused by the pressures put on us by our changing biology, cultural roles, and family expectations so that by the time we're five years old we begin to wobble through life based on the mixed signals we had to attempt to translate in order to survive. For the most part, we don't really succeed in learning new signals as we mature. No wonder we're confused!

I have observed in my workshops and in private consulting that boys brought up predominantly by women (women-trained males) learn to adapt their behavior to accommodate women. On the way, however, they usually suppress some very *normal* male behavior that is frowned upon by women. As a result, these boys grow into men who tend to know how to please women but seem unable to discover what it takes to please themselves. They also have difficulty in relating to other men and usually lack close male friends.

Women who have been brought up in an environment with a dominant father or an abundance of brothers (male-trained women) also adapt to their circumstances. Such girls learn to be "one of the boys." They learn to suppress giggles, crying, or talking "too much," and they learn to look down on other girls who behave that way. As a consequence, they too grow up knowing how to compete with or please men but have difficulty in pleasing themselves. They tend to look to men for approval and validation of their own self-worth, and they usually require an enormous amount of male attention, both quantitatively and qualitatively. As women, they also have few or no close female friends.

As children of indoctrination, we are usually unaware of the "conditioning" we experience, and we may actually believe that we need a new way of behaving. Men sometimes tell me that they don't like the "macho" talk in the workshop. I discovered that men who make that comment are concerned (on some level) that a woman might overhear such a conversation and would think badly of them. Granted, some macho talk is suppressive and demeaning, and some isn't. Being able to distinguish *healthy* expression or suppression is important in avoiding unnecessary conflicts.

CHAPTER SUMMARY

Men and women are very different biologically, and the differences are not limited to our sexual identity.

Equality will be established through a growing awareness of our individual needs, compassion for our differences, and sensitivity to our individual rights.

Physically predetermined differences between male and female behavior have not been identified in their proper context and may be the solution to most relationship "problems."

Biological functions translate into different perceptions and therefore different solutions.

We need compassion for ourselves and others in order to look for the "gift" that may be hiding in a perceived limitation.

Gender modes and codes affect our attitudes, emotions, decisions, and solutions.

Children have genders, too.

Knowing physical and emotional limits is very important to the male development.

Male-trained or female-trained individuals have learned to adapt their behavior to the dominant role model.

The ability to distinguish healthy expression or suppression is important in avoiding unnecessary conflicts.

4

HIS AND HERS: THE BODY OVERVIEW

Ignorance or lack of awareness of the biological differences between males and females can be very dangerous. One example is the recent study of a newly discovered hormone (DHEAS) that reduces the risk of heart disease in men and contributes to their longevity. Receiving this hormone apparently had the opposite effect on women. When administered to them, it actually accelerated their risk of heart disease rather than reducing it.

As genetic research continues to advance, we will all benefit from the plethora of knowledge it produces. Since 1959, over 3,300 inherited disorders—ranging from color blindness to diabetes—have been identified. Victor A. McKusick, M.D., author of *The Mendelian Inheritance in Man,* which many consider to be the bible of geneticists, suggests that even these 3,300 disorders may represent only fifteen percent of the genetically transmitted conditions. Yet almost all of us are quick to accuse each other of indulging in certain behavior that may actually be gender based, and over which we may have little or no control.

THE MASKED MEN OF MEDICINE

The fields of medicine and medical research were developed primarily by men. Because men dominated the profession, *male* biology was considered *human* biology until fairly recently. Women's bodies were compared to what was then the recognized standard in the industry: the male body. Women's particular aches and pains, P.M.S., menopause, and the like did not seem to warrant the same attention and depth of study as male bodies and male symptoms. Fortunately, this attitude is changing, but many women are still uncomfortable when talking about symptoms that might be interpreted by men (or male-trained women) as signs of weakness or being "too much like a woman."

As awareness of female needs increases, more emphasis will be given to female biology. As more women enter higher levels of the medical, psychiatric, and psychological professions, female conditions that were formerly demeaned as "women's problems" (or worse, "women's complaints") are attaining more credible status in medical research, diagnosis, and treatment.

Another example of the male orientation in medicine was found as recently as 1973 in the *Taber's Cyclopedic Medical Dictionary.* The dictionary defined "clitoris" as "homologous [similar in fundamental structure and in origin but not necessarily in function] to the penis of the male." In the definition of "penis" no mention is made of the clitoris, nor even the assertion that the penis is homologous to the clitoris. The dictionary illustrated the male penis, but no illustrations of either the clitoris or the vagina appeared. Whoever wrote the definition of "penis" also explained to the reader that the size of the penis would not affect the sexual satisfaction of either the male or the female, a surprising piece of information to be included in a definition. Want to guess if the definition was written by a man or woman? In checking in a number of recent medical dictionaries, with the exception of the reference to size, the same circumstance prevailed.

According to a 1984 report in the *Annals of Internal Medicine,* men with symptoms of heart disease are ten times more likely to be recommended for coronary bypass surgery than women with similar symptoms. The study involved 390 patients treated in New York City between July 1982, and June 1983. It found that even after accounting for differences in age and severity of disease, men were still considered for surgery almost seven times more often than women. The study also revealed that women are twice as likely as men to have their symptoms (such as chest pain and shortness of breath) dismissed as something other than heart disease by their doctors.

These researchers also found a significant difference in the reasons given by physicians for recommending further tests. With men, the physicians were most often attempting to determine the severity of the illness. With women, they were usually attempting to confirm the presence of disease.

None of these differences in recommended treatment were related to the occurrence rate of heart disease by gender. The findings show instead how social perceptions often mask scientific fact. Unfortunately, sexism is just as common in medicine as it is everywhere else.

THE GENETIC STRENGTH OF THE "WEAKER SEX"

If the male is considered to be the recognized "standard," women by comparison appear as the "weaker sex." This may be true in certain aspects, but when total comparisons are made, physical and emotional advantages begin to appear in favor of the female. Consider: Sperm carrying the male sex chromosome travel faster and have more "staying power" than sperm carrying the female sex chromosome, resulting in 120–140 males conceived for every 100 females.

Testosterone levels increase in the woman's system if a male is conceived. The uterine lining becomes thicker with a male embryo than it does with a female in an attempt to protect the expectant mother from the increased testosterone level which would otherwise produce in her secondary male characteristics such as coarse, darker hair and smaller breasts. The male embryo and its accompanying male hormones becomes a mild antibody to the expectant mother. (As only one out of the diverse array of questions this raises, what effect might this early alienation from the mother have on the emotional separation that males later establish with females?)

More males are spontaneously aborted during pregnancy than females. There are 106 male births for every 100 female births. More male babies than females are born dead, and thirty percent more males than females die within the first three months. Seventy percent of all birth defects are associated with males.

Testosterone acts as a general depressor of the immune system, which means that a male child is unequally vulnerable to leukemia, cancers of the lymphatic system, respiratory ailments, hepatitis, and gastrointestinal illnesses. A female, however, has more genetic adaptability related to the sex chromosome, because the Y chromosome is basically an empty chromosome. That means that if a recessive character is found in the genetic material of the X chromosome, the male will have the symptom, while a female may not.

As a result of the hormone levels in the male fetus, boy babies are born less sturdy and less ready for the world than girls. Though males are about five percent heavier than females at birth, male babies are four to six weeks behind female babies in physical maturity. The fontanel (the soft spot on the top of the head that later forms the skull to protect the brain) remains open longer in boys. Bone ossification and dental maturity are achieved earlier in girls. Girls sit, crawl, walk, and talk earlier. In effect, boys are born "prematurely" if compared with girls. Boys begin to catch up (physically) with girls when they reach puberty, although puberty appears several years later in boys than girls. By puberty, the number of surviving males and females is equal.

Perhaps as we mature as a species, the question of who is better or weaker will disappear. Compassion and appreciation may replace judgment as we recognize our natural differences.

CHAPTER SUMMARY

Ignorance or unawareness of the biological differences between males and females can be very dangerous.

Until recently, *male* biology was considered *human* biology.

As awareness of female needs increases, more emphasis is being given to female biology.

Men with symptoms of heart disease are ten times more likely to be recommended for coronary bypass surgery than women with similar symptoms.

Social perceptions often mask scientific fact.

When total comparisons are made, physical and emotional advantages appear to be in favor of the female.

Between 120–140 males are conceived for every 100 females.

A male embryo and its accompanying male hormones becomes a mild antibody to the expectant mother.

Male babies are four to six weeks behind female babies in physical maturity.

Girls sit, crawl, walk, and talk earlier than boys.

Bone ossification and dental maturity are achieved earlier in girls.

A male child is unequally vulnerable to leukemia, cancers of the lymphatic system, respiratory ailments, hepatitis, and gastrointestinal illnesses.

Boys begin to catch up (physically) with girls when they reach puberty.

By puberty, males and females are equal in number.

5

HOW THE BIOLOGICAL
DIFFERENCES AFFECT BEHAVIOR

The differences in male and female biology are often overlooked when explanations are sought for cultural, socialized, or emotional behavior. How many of us, for example, are aware of the difference in hearing sensitivity between men and women? Men don't hear as clearly as women, and this fact certainly should be taken into account when women feel that men are always talking too loud, being too boisterous, or trying to dominate by using too much demand in their voices. Alternately, of course, men often feel that women talk too softly, lack assertiveness, or are trying to be seductive by talking just above a whisper. The vocal chords of men and women are designed differently. Knowing the differences, however, still doesn't give us license to self-righteously state them to one another and then go on to indulge in inconsiderate behavior. Quite the opposite: Men might strive to become more sensitive to women's hearing levels and realize that they needn't talk as loudly to women as they do to men. And women might appreciate that they may need to talk a little louder so that their voices are easier for men to hear, even though the current volume of their conversation sounds perfectly loud enough to them. When she is with other women, a woman can relax and return to a more natural level; a man can return to his natural volume when he's with other men. This same consideration applies to our difference in sensitivities to taste, touch, and smell.

BIOLOGICAL UNDERPINNINGS

Baby girls are more sensitive to touch, more responsive to light, have a keener sense of smell, are less fretful, and undergo a different process of development of the nervous system than do baby boys.

Baby girls smile more, eat less, and control their bladders and bowels earlier.

These characteristics develop before the child has had a chance to be trained or "socialized," and even in the nursery, females are more sensitive than males. Gender identification has already begun.

This gender identification seems to continue and expand as we grow. As early as kindergarten, our gender identification has already been well established. In her book, *Boys and Girls: Superheroes in the Doll Corner,* Vivian Gussin Paley looks at the way boys and girls play their games. She used the familiar game of "Let's Pretend" as a basis for observing the children in her classroom. For over a year she recorded how the children talked, played, fantasized, and acted with each other. She was surprised to find that some of her expectations of different behavior just didn't happen. Little girls ran around more than she expected, were at least as messy, and were just as likely to be quarrelsome as the boys. The little boys also cried more than she expected. It was when the children began play acting that the gender identification became more obvious.

Even though Paley tried to change the children's stereotypical behavior, the little boys always adopted masculine roles of heroes, monsters, villains. The little girls became the mothers, babies, and princesses. She observed that when it was time for free play, the girls immediately went to the arts and crafts tables while the boys went to work on the blocks. Even while she was reading stories, the boys and girls, by their own decision, sat on opposite sides of the circle.

The need for a child to be identified as a male or female is very strong. Paley realized that no amount of pressure applied by herself or other adults seemed to change the children's need for separation and definition of sex roles. She concluded that the children really believe that they invented the differences and are bound to prove that these differences do in fact exist.

A cross-cultural study of 201 societies indicated that cooking was an exclusively female activity in 158 of them and exclusively male in only 5. Hunting in 179 societies was exclusively male and never exclusively female. Males almost always had exclusive involvement in lumbering, metalwork, house building, fishing, and making musical instruments. Females were responsible for weaving, food preparation, childcare, and preparing narcotic drinks.

It has been established that even isolated societies engage in typical male/female role behavior. Slight variations might exist in how the roles are expressed, but the separations are evident.

My consulting and research implies an instinctual internal need exists for males and females to identify themselves by gender. We operate according to the commonly held belief that little boys and girls are *taught* the differences by unenlightened outsiders. At my workshops, the prevailing notion is that men and women behave differently because of our "training." Almost everyone seems to believe this theory without question, and we are quick to point to "macho" role models (for men) and "submissive" role models for women. While *all* powerful role models do not support these two particular images of man and woman, in our behavior we tend to ignore what the positive models have conveyed to us. What happened, for example, to all the little boys who were brought up on "Father Knows Best," "The Donna Reed Show," and "Lassie," just three of the many successful and "positive" television programs? These remarkably popular series each featured a male parent who was compassionate, considerate, loving, and sensitive. While staunchly fulfilling the cultural role model of "breadwinner," these fathers never raised their voices at their wives or children; never resorted to physical violence; avoided or resolved conflicts with other males in positive ways; and never failed to be appropriately dressed, showered, and shaved. If we are to attribute our gender-like behavior solely to our role models, why is it that we don't include the "positive" examples we received as well?

I suggest that children become confused about how to behave "appropriately" because their parents either overemphasize the differences between men and women (positively or negatively) or because they attempt to ignore the differences.

As Paley discovered in her research, despite attempts to alter stereotypes, five-year-olds were more comfortable in their gender-based roles. I am not proposing that we submit to limited possibilities based on gender, nor do I believe that we should tolerate inappropriate behavior because of gender. I am suggesting that once we know our *biological foundation,* we have a better chance to redirect our lives. Our biology may set the stage, but our intelligence and compassion can help us rewrite the play.

NO, WE DON'T SEE EYE-TO-EYE

Eight percent of all men have color perception problems, while only .5 percent of women have difficulty perceiving colors. That translates into 8 out of 100 men, as opposed to 1 out of 200 women, or 16 to 1. (Does this explain the average man's appreciation for black, brown, and gray?)

Color perception is a functional, measurable difference between males and females. This means that a subtle color difference which appears obvious to a woman may go unnoticed by a man.

The following conversation could be about almost any subject when two people have a different perception. Does this sound familiar?:

She says, "So which color do you think would go with this couch?"

He says, "Either one is fine."

She says, "This is important. I want your opinion about this!"

He says, "I told you, I don't care! They look about the same to me!"

Then she seethes, and he looks exasperated.

Unfortunately this conversation is repeated over and over again. Most of us have been able to refine it to the point where the conversation usually ends quickly to avoid the obvious escalation, though it almost always succeeds in isolating us from one another. To the man, the woman may appear to be overly sensitive, too picky, or just making a big deal out of nothing. To the woman, the man may appear insensitive, defensive, and/or disturbingly indifferent. In any case, such an exchange shows how internal (and usually inaccurate) assumptions are made based on individual experiential perception and interpretation, then stored as fact.

For example, the woman, not knowing that a man may not be able to see any significant difference, could assume that the man was deliberately not choosing one color over another because he wanted her to know how unimportant he thinks the issue is. She believes he may be avoiding a decision so that if the color doesn't work he can blame her! This is another bit of evidence to her of his unwillingness to make the kind of decisions that she feels are significant.

The man, on the other hand, may decide that the woman is deliberately trying to intimidate him by pointing out an area (color difference) that he is uneasy about or does not understand. Or he may think she is being absurdly sensitive about an issue that is obviously (to him) insignificant. He decides that she doesn't understand priorities and wastes time on trivial items. He stores this misinformation as fact.

If they want to avoid the escalation of this conversation beyond its importance, both parties will back off, submit, or remove themselves to avoid further controversy. Each person in this example loses, and each assumes he or she is the loser in the interaction. Communication is a complex process that is made even more difficult by these types of assumptions.

Men and women are also significantly different in the way they visually perceive. In the Thomas Water Level Task Report, 100% of college males indicated the correct water level within 2 degrees in a tilted flask while only 31% of the females did; 69% of the females were 15–20 degrees off. This flask task was conducted with males as young as twelve years of age, and the accuracy was consistent. It's not surprising to note that this study is quite popular, because it was presumed (from a social or "nurturing" point of view) that women would have had more experience in pouring water. Even so, 69% of the women got it consistently wrong. Of the men, 100% were right.

Men have better daylight vision than women but worse nighttime vision. This difference intensifies as men get older. It is interesting, though, that men usually assume the nighttime driving task.

Females are less sensitive to light than males. Male infants respond to what is visually interesting in their environments: lights, patterns, three-dimensional objects. Boys are drawn to objects rather than people. Girls respond preferentially to the people in their environment.

They find faces much more interesting than objects. These differences in interest appear in the crib, long before parental attitudes or socialization can affect the infant.

Males are measurably better than females at visual tasks, maps, mazes, three-dimensional rotation, and sense of direction; they are also better at orienting themselves in space.

HAVE WOMEN BEEN FRAMED?

A woman's pelvis is designed for child bearing, which also causes a woman's hips to sway, another significant gender identification. Her female configuration makes running and climbing ladders more difficult for her than for a male. Women's joints are looser than men's; therefore, women are *more flexible and limber,* while men have thicker bone structures and can thus withstand greater outside impact. When compared with those of men, most female shoulders are narrower, while their hips are wider. Women have smaller hands, weaker thumbs, a thinner skull, and lighter bones than men do.

As a result, it is easy for men to say, "That's no big deal! Why don't you just open the jar?" A man's grip is a lot stronger than a woman's. The male thumb can be as much as twenty times stronger than a female's, and the size of his hands gives him advantages in many tasks. What appears to be dainty indulgence on the woman's part actually reflects the limits of her physical structure.

Female skulls on an average are smaller at the base, but larger in circumference at the crown, and women have a more vertical forehead than men.

Females have stiffer lips than males, and women's eyes take up more face area than men's.

Women have higher pitched voices (shorter vocal chords) and smaller lungs than men.

THICK SKINNED OR THICK SKIN

Men have fewer nerve endings on their skin and more hair on their body for protection than women do. A man's skin is thicker and less prone to bruising, and a woman's skin is more sensitive to touch. Soft fabrics are therefore much more important to a woman's comfort than to a man's.

A woman's upper body has less strength than a man's, even if their degree of physical fitness is comparable. On average, women are 10% shorter, 20% less muscular, and half as strong as men in the arms.

The amount and method of storing fat is quite different for men and women. Men on an average have 15% body fat, and women have 23%. Since fat is the fuel of our bodies, this 8% difference is a major factor in the amount of energy and stamina women have as opposed to that of men. Imagine your own body either increasing or decreasing in size overnight by 8%. How might this affect your activities for the day?

Not only does the amount of fat differ, but the way the fat is stored differs. Estrogen works positively and negatively for women. The good news is that when women eat and metabolize, estrogen breaks down the fat and stores it in two different ways. First, women have the same soft fat that men have, which provides immediate glucose for immediate strength and immediate use of energy, if she needs it. Second, the estrogen slows down her metabolism so that she stores what is called "harder fat" all over her body. When a man runs out of his 15% energy under strenuous conditions, he has depleted his available glucose. When women run out of available glucose, estrogen begins breaking down the harder fat, which allows the woman to "outlast" the man. The bad news is that her system stores the fat, and she can't lose it as fast as a man can. A man loses more weight sitting still than a woman does because his muscle-to-fat ratio is higher. Muscle mass burns more calories than fat, and because a man has a higher ratio of muscle, he burns approximately five calories an hour more than a woman.

Women have more insulating fat under their skins and are therefore less sensitive to cold and more buoyant in water than men are. Women are more susceptible to the effects of alcohol, and are more likely to incur physical damage from alcohol abuse than men. Women who try to drink as much alcohol as a male counterpart may be affected twice as much by the same number of drinks.

DECODING SKILLS

Women tend to dream of indoor scenes, and other women are prominent in their dreams. Interactions are usually friendly, with little overt sexual content. The faces in a woman's dreams are usually more recognizable than those in a man's. Men's dreams contain more confrontation with strangers and more highlights of physical violence. And in men's dreams, males outnumber women by two to one; when women enter the dream, it is usually in a sexual context.

Boys are more physically aggressive, fight more, and daydream more actively than girls.

Girls are better at grasping verbal concepts, at making analogies, and at all language comprehension.

Girls speak at an earlier age, have better enunciation, and are generally better readers. Earlier verbal skills give females an advantage in school at a young age. Males catch up when math becomes an important part of school activity.

The right hemisphere of the brain (spatial talents) develops as early as six years in males and as late as thirteen in females.

Young girls draw *people* first, boys focus on drawing *objects*. Many of the nurses who have taken my workshop have confirmed that when they want a baby girl to relax or stop crying, they pick her up, touch her, talk to her. When they want the same for a baby boy, they give him objects to look at and hold.

Four-year-old girls have more advanced cell growth in the left hemisphere of the brain (verbal) than four-year-old boys. Males have greater development on the right side (spatial).

Girls are more aggressive with words; boys more aggressive physically. Males apparently find large muscular movement satisfying and rewarding, which may be linked to testosterone and the resulting increase in sensitivity to threat and physical contact.

There is a greater incidence of learning disabilities in males than in females. It is presumed that the problem is caused by the lower level of brain symmetry in males.

In 16 repeated studies, women were more empathic than men. In 75 studies, women were superior to men in decoding nonverbal cues.

Women are better at language skills: fluency, verbal reasoning, written prose, and reading.

Women sing in tune six times more frequently than males do. (Shouldn't we now have a little more compassion for men who don't want to sing in public?)

THE NOSE KNOWS

Females are much more sensitive to pheromones (scent messages, a form of scent communication) than males.

For both men and women, the sense of smell is duller in the morning, keener at night. But whatever time of day, women have a better sense of smell than men, according to two researchers who explained this olfactory discrepancy between sexes. Robert Henkin of Georgetown University believes that smell sensitivity is linked to hormone levels in the body. When ovulation occurs and estrogen levels rise, olfactory sensitivity soars—up to 1,000 times. Henkin's findings suggest a hormonal basis for women's olfactory gifts and a possible link to reproduction. Females with no ovaries had a decreased level of sense of smell.

To a statistically significant degree, mothers of six hour-old babies can find their own baby among others by smell alone. Males cannot. How many times have men and women argued over the "odor" of food, clothing, environment, and hygiene? How many times has a woman told a man that something was old, spoiled, or smelly? The man will pick up the plate or the carton of milk or the piece of clothing and sniff it. He needs to do this before he can make his judgment, and even then the smell will not be as strong to him as it is to her. The man thinks that the woman is too picky or overly critical, and the woman thinks the man is indulgent, stubborn, and inconsiderate. He may not realize that the odor is offensive, and she cannot deny her experience (even though the man expects her to).

STOKING THE BODY FURNACE

Males and females do not process food in the same way. The differences in our brain organization, muscle mass, and hormones directly affect the way food is metabolized in our bodies. An example of this was found in nutritional studies by medical researcher Elsie M. Widdowson. In 1946, her attention was focused on the relative strengths and weaknesses of the postwar European men and women. She found that over 60% of the undernourished patients were male.

In 1947, Widdowson examined hundreds of orphaned German children. This group of children had been surviving solely on war rations. The German children, in comparison to the American and British children of the same age, were shorter and weighed less. She noted that the older children suffered more than the younger children, but in all age groups the boys showed more effects of deprivation than the girls.

In research with animals (as a member of the Department of Medicine at Cambridge University), Widdowson discovered that males and females metabolize proteins and fats at different rates. By causing deprivation, she found that the males lost 16% of their body protein and 19% of their body fat. The females, on the other hand, lost 8% body protein and 37% body fat. Females have greater stores of body fat and are therefore able to withstand food deprivation for longer periods of time.

In addition, when allowed to eat as much as they wanted, the females were able to recover normal body protein and fat levels but the males did not. Female fat storage differences increase at puberty and increase even more so after the first pregnancy. The assumption is that the additional fat allows a mother to survive longer, thereby being able to supply stored nutrients to her young. Males grow faster and larger than females during puberty and therefore need more food.

Widdowson's evidence shows that throughout our lives, in every stage of our growth, males and females have different dietary needs. I think it is very important for us to understand these differences and begin to design our nutrition around our individual needs.

Men are 40% muscle, 15% fat. Women are 23% muscle, 25% fat. Men have striated (high fiber) muscles. Women have smooth (less fiber) muscles. Striated muscle is more "defined" and burns more calories than smooth muscle. Men's bodies have a higher muscle-to-fat ratio than women's. Striated muscles also burn fat at a higher rate, which provides but also diminishes immediate available glucose. The effects of this gender difference on males is described in Chapter 9, "Allocation of Energy."

Male hormones encourage fat accumulation mainly above the waist, while female hormones cause fat to accumulate in the hips and thighs, possibly to store energy for use during pregnancy and milk production.

The fat accumulation in the male (located higher in the body) makes him more prone to heart stress and heart disease. The fat cells in the stomach region increase in size to store fat. This also gives some men the body shape of an orange on a toothpick. For the woman, fat cells in the hips and thighs increase in *number* to store fat. It is easier to shrink the stomach fat cells than to lose the added hip and thigh cells.

Women's skin is tethered to the underlying muscle by thin, parallel cords, much like the construction of a mattress. These cords don't have much "give," however. Excess fat fills in the valleys between the cords, then shows through the skin, creating an orange peel effect known as cellulite. Men's muscle connectors, on the other hand, are a tightly crisscrossed maze of strands. His fat accumulates in one smooth layer, because there are no valleys or ridges in which it can collect.

Women experience temperature changes and feel colder more often than men, even though they have more "insulation" in the form of body fat. Body warmth depends on two main factors: the ability to generate heat and the ability to keep from losing it. Men are at a slightly better advantage than women in generating heat. Given the fact that the average male has 40% muscle mass compared to the average 23% in females, his metabolic rate (an important predictor of body heat production) is higher. Men's body fat is more evenly distributed along the torso, which is a big advantage in keeping the body insulated against the cold. The average woman's higher proportion of body fat (25% vs. 15%) helps protect her from losing heat. However, the benefits of better insulation are somewhat lost by the woman's poorer circulation and lower metabolic rate.

Women seem to have a significantly wider range of temperatures at which their bodies are comfortable than men do. The male body temperature is usually 98.6 degrees, with only slight variations from one man to the next. For women, body temperature may vary from the normal 98.6 degrees by as much as three to five degrees during a month. This fluctuation is partly due to varying hormone levels, specifically the rise and fall of estrogen in a woman's body during her menstrual cycle. Before a woman ovulates, her normal resting temperature drops to an average of about 96 degrees, then rises at least half a degree following ovulation. Some women who have been "cold-blooded" all their lives become much less sensitive to chilly temperatures after they enter menopause because their bodies produce fewer hormones.

Temperature preferences between men and women have become more apparent now that the genders work together as well as live together. That's partly due to the fact that men's traditional office attire (pants, long-sleeved shirts, and jackets) is consistently heavier than women's. Women feel the cold more acutely because blood leaves the extremities to protect the central body core more quickly. They feel colder because the temperature of their hands and feet has actually dropped abruptly. Women can counteract and possibly eliminate this sensitivity to cold by vigorous exercise, which increases the body's metabolic rate for hours afterward and can increase the body's ability to produce heat by more than 15 times. (Men can also become more sensitive to a woman's changing body temperature and to her need to fluctuate room temperature.)

Altering one's diet can also assist the body's furnace. In general, both men and women feel much warmer after eating, because the body's metabolic rate is slightly higher. Carbohydrates, such as bread and potatoes, trigger more heat production than do fatty foods, such as bacon, which block heat production. Supplementing body fluids with our choice of beverages also plays a part in maintaining a sense of warmth. It seems that coffee should warm the body, but in the long run, it makes the drinker feel colder. Caffeine, a diuretic, encourages fluid loss; as a vasoconstrictor, caffeine inhibits the flow of blood throughout the body (nicotine has a similar effect). Water and fruit juices are much safer because there are no side effects.

PROCREATION PROGRAMMING

Most of us are familiar with characteristics of the sex hormones. We know that at puberty they influence hair growth, breast and muscle development, and our attraction to the opposite sex. We have some knowledge about the effect of various hormones when they are taken by athletes or transsexuals or others who attempt to manipulate body development. What is not very clear is the *organizational* effects of these hormones.

Organizational effects are genetically programmed into the organism long before puberty, in fact, as already noted, at various stages of the fetus' development in the womb. These organizational effects not only alter the form and shape the body will have, but also the way the body will respond to hormonal influences at puberty.

People with bass voices have more testosterone and less estrogen than tenors; they also have a more active sex life. Rapists and exhibitionists have higher testosterone levels than normal. Alcoholics have lower testosterone levels.

Some studies have shown that tall male executives have sex more frequently than short male executives, and that their level of testosterone may increase both before and after sex. Older men produce more estrogen and less testosterone than younger men. Older men are more patient and are potentially better lovers because they have to be. The ability to ejaculate a number of times is replaced by snuggling, conversation, and other forms of foreplay.

The differences between estrogen and testosterone are still being investigated. Basically, we know that testosterone is a male hormone responsible for a number of effects, including aggression, competition, deeper and more forceful voices, hair coarseness, and the like. Estrogen is a roller coaster hormone that affects mood change (P.M.S.), fat storage, and egg production. The effects of estrogen cannot be predicted as easily as the effects of testosterone.

As noted earlier, the woman's immune system (because of the XX chromosome) functions at a higher level than a man's. However, there are negative aspects to be considered. The female immune system is so efficient that it sometimes attacks the body it is supposed to protect. Women suffer much more than men do from autoimmune diseases (multiple sclerosis, juvenile-onset diabetes, rheumatoid arthritis, and Graves disease).

Systemic lupus affects about 500,000 people in the United States, of which more than 450,000 are women. According to researchers, the disease is often extremely difficult to diagnose because some of the symptoms (depression, obsessional neurosis, or schizophrenia) are often misdiagnosed as psychological problems.

Mother Nature protects women for the purpose of motherhood, whether or not as individuals, they want to have children. Men are genetically programmed to be hunters and sex-seekers, whether or not as individuals, they hunt or seek sex. Estrogen and progesterone give women that "glow," self-assurance, and readiness for procreation. Testosterone in men induces confidence and the necessary aggression for pursuit.

To measure the effects of hormones, one study observed 42 children whose mothers had been given steroid hormones during pregnancy. Each of the children had a brother or sister who had not been exposed to the hormones; these "control" brothers and sisters could then be used as a comparison group. The researchers found significant personality differences in the two groups. The children who had been exposed to progestins (which act like male hormones) scored consistently higher on traits considered masculine than their brothers and sisters of the same sex. That is, they were more independent, individualistic, self-assured, and self-sufficient. Children who had been exposed to estrogens, particularly synthetic diethylstilbestrol (DES), scored higher on feminine characteristics: more group-oriented and more interested in relationship and communication skills.

This research supports the premise that many of our differences in perception, cognition, and personality are gender-based and a result of biological differences that appear, at least on the surface, to be relatively minor.

June Reinisch, developmental psychobiologist, conducted a study of 4,653 infants which indicated that the length of pregnancy has a significant effect on how quickly infants progress to sitting, crawling, and standing; and found that baby boys and girls generally reach these stages on different timetables. These early developmental areas correlate with psychological characteristics normally associated with adult males and adult females.

For example, little girls sit up without support earlier than boys, but spend more time sitting before they stand with support than little boys do. Boys may start to crawl earlier than girls, but they crawl for a longer period of time before they walk with support. Perhaps sitting allows the little girls more face-to-face interaction, and crawling allows boys separation and independence. In a sense, the boy is already "hunting," and the girl is already "socializing."

In the early 1970's, when psychologists Eleanor Maccoby and Carol Jacklin analyzed studies and looked for sex differences in behavior, they found a clear-cut difference in male and female aggression. In every culture, boys were more physically aggressive than girls. The data also showed that boys are more likely than girls to imagine themselves reacting to conflict with physical aggression.

Research indicates that prenatal (in the womb) exposure to masculinizing hormones often makes girls act more like boys in various ways. But the effect in boys was even greater, which surprised the researchers. Based on animal studies, researchers assumed that any hormones with masculinizing properties, in addition to those normally produced by the male fetus, would not influence behavior. However, the studies suggested that if higher levels of these hormones reached boys' brains before birth, the differences between male and female would be even greater.

Research with monkeys has shown that dominant males have higher levels of the sex hormone testosterone than other monkeys and that they are more sexually active.

Evidence suggests that men who achieve a rise in status through their own efforts and who feel good about the result, experience an accompanying rise in their hormone levels. Dominant men who showed high testosterone levels also showed higher levels of prolactin (a stress hormone) which indicated an increase in anxiety. The simultaneous increase of the two hormones is like stepping on the accelerator and brake at the same time because prolactin is thought to inhibit the sexual dominance that testosterone delivers.

This evidence also suggests that being at the top of the pile in human society not only produces a feeling of dominance (with its accompanying hormone changes) in having arrived there, but also causes a sense of anxiety related to the fears of how one is going to stay there. The prolactin change indicates a shift in anxiety that takes place whether or not the male is aware of it.

"Men give love to get sex, and women give sex to get love." This statement has a ring of truth to it because of our genetic design and evolution.

Since human females, like those of most species, make a relatively large investment in the production and survival of each child (and males can sometimes get away with a relatively small investment), women

Biological Differences Summary

Females

Less hair covering
Skin bruises more easily
.5% color perception problems
Better nighttime vision
Sweat glands more evenly distributed
Joints more flexible
Lighter bones
Smaller hands, weaker thumbs
23% muscle
25% fat
Burn less calories
Evenly distributed fat layer
Wrinkle earlier
Better oxygen supply to the brain
Sit, crawl, walk, and talk sooner
Babies less fretful, smile more, eat
    less, control bladder earlier
Up to 40% more connectors in the
    brain, larger corpus collosum
Spatial talents develop at age 13
At 60 years of age have 90% of
    strength and flexibility of age 20
More susceptible to alcohol abuse
Larger lower brain (emotions)
Advanced cell growth in verbal
    hemisphere at age 4

Males

Fewer nerve endings
Thicker skin
8% color perception problems
Better daytime vision
Larger lungs
Joints are tighter
Thicker skull
10% taller
40% muscle
15% fat
50% stronger arms
Less buoyant in water
Hair more coarse
Greater incidence of learning disorders
Weaker immune system
Babies spontaneously aborted, born
    dead or blind
30% more die in first 3 months
75% dyslexics are male
Spatial talents develop at age 6
At 60 years of age have 60% of
    strength and flexibility of age 20
90% of those diagnosed hyperactive
Skulls larger at base, smaller at crown

approach sex and reproduction in extremely different ways than men do. While we evolved together as a single species, the sexual needs and tendencies that proved to be reproductive success for one sex probably spelled reproductive disaster for the other.

A man can produce more reproductive cells in two seconds than a woman can in her entire lifetime. (And he is capable of doing this a number of times a day.) One explanation of why women tend to marry older men is that while younger men can produce more sexual activity than older men, an older man can provide enough active sperm for reproduction and at the same time, at least ostensibly, provide greater stability and protection for her offspring. As women become more independent (less at the mercy of economics and child rearing), their selection criteria for a mate may change. Women may select younger men who tend to provide greater energy in the relationship, greater flexibility (older men tend to get "set in their ways"), and more compatible physical stamina (not only sexually, but in exercising, working, and playing).

Women often exhibit physiological arousal when watching sex films or listening to erotic tapes. But a woman does not always feel aroused at the same time as a man. There is a built-in time lapse between the response of her body and the conscious part of her brain. She is protected by nature from making snap decisions that could result in pregnancy.

That doesn't mean she can't or shouldn't be instantly attracted to a man, and it doesn't mean that she can't or shouldn't pursue numbers of sexual partners. What it does mean is that the attraction (or repulsion) she feels may not be purely physical. She may be reacting to the effect of evolutionary programming that is meant to protect her, but this is not necessarily evolutionary protection for the man. Quite the contrary!

A number of studies show that a woman is less likely to experience orgasm during a "one-night-stand" than when she is functioning in the context of a stable, long-term relationship.

The regulating hormones (L.H. and F.S.H.) in both men and women determine sex drive. They are constantly present in the male, and his hormone levels rise and fall many times during the day. In women, hormone levels synchronize the ovulation and menstruation cycles. Only during ovulation do these hormones work together to increase her readiness for sex (and also increase her sense of sight, taste, and smell). Pheromones (smell messages) travel to the hypothalamus and to other areas of the brain known to be involved in sex. During puberty, the apocrine glands in the breasts, armpits, and pubic skin alter moods and attraction between men and women, even when there is no awareness of scent or odor.

A man's sexual drive increases significantly after puberty, reaching its height before the age of twenty. A man reaches full reproductive maturity between the ages of 19 and 24. From then on, his sex drive steadily declines toward zero, which generally occurs after the age of 70. A woman's drive increases very slowly after puberty. She doesn't reach her sexual peak until around the age of 28, and she then remains at the same level until she is around 45, when a slow decline begins.

For the woman, orgasm is a potential. Orgasm is not necessary for her to reproduce. It is, however, necessary for the male! Orgasm in women is not a universally known phenomenon. There are a few cultures where no word exists for the female orgasm since no orgasm is expected. In the United States, 5–10% percent of women never experience orgasm, and another 30–40% experience it only occasionally.

The pleasure of orgasm is the motivating reproductive force for the male, and when he has reached orgasm, his biological drive is satisfied. It is generally the older, more mature male who can prolong his arousal and thereby increase his partner's satisfaction.

The Hite Report showed that an overwhelming number of women chose affection, intimacy, and love, not orgasm, as their primary enjoyment during intercourse. Further, most women considered the moment of penetration to be their favorite physical sensation.

In sexual matters, the woman has a greater investment in time, in commitment, and in physical vulnerability than the man. Because her involvement is *major,* she needs and deserves greater control in choices about birth control and reproduction. The care, nurturing, and survival of the young is a long-term commitment. The female always knows who the mother is (herself), and she can usually determine who the father is. That father must then supply her needs in order to maintain her faithfulness, or he risks not being able to continue his genetic line.

In the next chapter, we'll be noting some of the differences in male/female brain functioning.

CHAPTER SUMMARY

The differences between male and female biology are often overlooked when explanations are sought for cultural, socialized, or emotional behavior.

Young children actively create separate male and female worlds in order to define themselves.

Even isolated societies engage in typical male/female role behavior.

Research implies an instinctual internal need for males and females to identify themselves by gender.

Once we know our *biological foundation,* we have a better chance to redirect our lives.

Communication between male and female is a complex process made even more difficult by inaccurate assumptions.

6

THE BRAIN—INTERPRETER OF OUR EXPERIENCE

Brain researcher and neuroscientist, Roger Gorski, said in an interview for "Films for the Humanities" that he had been studying hundreds of brains, and that until he placed male and female brains side by side, he had not looked for distinctions. For example, he points out that the hypothalamus in males is five times larger than in females. Since that time, he has been amazed by the number of differences between male and female brains.

The brain is the most complex and sophisticated part of the human body. Many scientists now attribute the development of human consciousness to the development and evolution of the corpus callosum, the mass of white transverse fibers con-

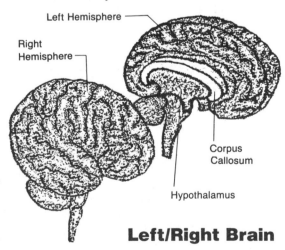

Left Hemisphere

Right Hemisphere

Corpus Callosum

Hypothalamus

Left/Right Brain

necting the cerebral hemispheres in higher mammals. Once the two halves of the brain could communicate with one another through the tiny bundles of nerves and fibers, consciousness emerged.

The brains of male and female mammals are not the same, either anatomically or in terms of connections between neurons. Recent brain research supports these statements.

Left and Right Mode Comparison

This is a general list of commonly accepted brain functions. Note: Research in this area is still sketchy, and there is evidence that this breakdown is not quite accurate, nor does it take into account the significant differences between the left and right hemispheres of men and women.

Left mode:	Right mode:
Verbal: Using words to name, describe, define things.	Nonverbal: Awareness of things, but very little connection with words.
Analytic: Figuring things out step-by-step and piece-by-piece.	Synthetic: Putting ideas together to form whole concepts.
Symbolic: Using a symbol to represent something. For example, "x" sign stands for the process of multiplication.	Concrete: Relating to things at the present moment.
Abstract: The ability to take a small bit of information and use it to represent the whole.	Analogic: Identifying likenesses between things; understanding metaphors.
Temporal: Keeping track of time; sequential, doing one thing at a time in the proper order.	Nontemporal: With no sense of time.
Rational: Determination based on reasons and facts.	Nonrational: Determination not based on facts or reason.
Digital: Ability to use numbers	Spatial: Knowing relationship of things and understanding how parts fit together.
Logical: Conclusions based on logic; one thing following another in logical order.	Intuitive: Understanding often based on incomplete information, hunches, feelings, or visual images.
Linear: Thinking in terms of associated ideas; one thought directly following another.	Holistic: Seeing the whole, all at once; perceiving the overall patterns and structures.

The corpus callosum is as much as 40% larger in women than it is in men. Brain researchers now assume that the larger the corpus callosum, the greater communication there is between the right and left hemispheres of the brain. To understand the significance of this discovery, we must understand how divided the brain is in its abilities.

THE MUSIC OF THE HEMISPHERES

Men tend to have stronger left-hemisphere brain functions than women. Males predominantly use the left side of the brain, where logic, reasoning, and rational thinking take place. The right side of the brain is responsible for abstract ideas, communication, relationship, and holistic approaches to solutions. Men tend to excel at math because they can "see" the abstract relationships better (left mode). Right-hemisphere functions are also accessible to men: They tend to make better baseball players than women because they can perceive the spatial relationship between ball and bat. Men tend to be more successful than women at reading maps because they are better at relating features on the map to objects in the real world. They're also usually better at packing the car for a family trip because of their ability to arrange three-dimensional objects in space.

With 40% more connections between the verbal left hemisphere and the spatial right hemisphere, women are better equipped to integrate "left- and right-brain thinking." Women also excel at skills related to the right hemisphere of the brain, such as verbal fluency and comprehension. They tend to talk better and to learn foreign languages more easily than men. They're also better at expressing their feelings in words—and more likely to do so than men.

In a study by neuropsychologist Sandra Witelson, a group of two hundred normal right-handed boys and girls between the ages of six and fourteen were blindfolded and given two objects to hold—one in their left hand and one in their right hand. The objects were then taken from the youngsters and mixed in with other similar items. The blindfolds were removed, and they were then asked to pick the objects they had held. Because sensory information from the left hand travels to the right hemisphere of the brain (and vice versa) and because the right hemisphere is known to control spatial skills, the expectation was that the children would be better at identifying the objects they held in their left hands. The boys performed as expected: more accurate in identifying the objects held in their left hands. The girls, however, were able to identify objects held in either hand with the same degree of accuracy. Apparently, the information transferred from the girls' left hemispheres much more efficiently than it did in the boys'.

When it comes to speaking and making hand movements that contribute to motor skills, the brain seems to be more focally (with limitation) organized in women than in men. This may explain the fact that girls generally speak earlier, articulate better, and also have better fine-motor control. (A larger portion of women than men are right-handed.) But when it comes to abstract tasks, such as *defining* words, women's brains are more diffusely organized than men's.

The greater size of the female corpus callosum indicates that women have more pathways for interactions between left and right hemispheres than men, and that men and women may use the same sides of the brain for different purposes. Women's highly developed corpus callosum allows them to better integrate reason and intuition and to search for harmony and balance.

A male's right hemisphere allows him to excel at spatial tasks, such as rotating three-dimensional images in his mind's eye and picturing what they look like on all sides. The basis for a woman's more specialized understanding of emotions and her ability to discern the meaning of facial expressions resides in the right brain.

THE PLUS AND MINUS BRAIN GAME

During the course of research by Doreen Kimura, who studied more than 100,000 intellectually-gifted youngsters, attempts were made to find a link between child-rearing practices and mathematical ability. No support was found for the various socialization hypotheses. The researchers did, however, find evidence for a biological explanation.

In most people, mathematical reasoning ability is probably stronger under the influence of the right hemisphere of the brain. And because left-handers tend to have an advantage at tasks related to the right hemisphere, it seemed reasonable to the researchers that left-handers would have an advantage in mathematical reasoning. As suspected, adolescents who scored extremely high on the mathematics test were much more likely to be left-handed.

As I noted earlier, research has suggested that left-handedness and immune disorders are related to high levels of testosterone and that the gender difference in mathematical reasoning ability may also be related to prenatal exposure to testosterone. Brains (as well as bodies) are formed by sex hormones. Structural brain differences are found in fetuses by the twenty-sixth week.

There are certain endorphins (chemicals produced and released in the brain) whose functions cause the body to react to stress, "fight or flight" situations, and sexual activity. Some endorphins exist in men that don't exist in women and vice versa. The effect of sex-related chemicals is still a new science and far from being fully understood.

Women tend to have more of the chemical serotonin, and men have more dopamine. "Depression" is diagnosed more often among females, and depression has been related to serotonin levels. On the other hand, schizophrenia is diagnosed more often among men, and schizophrenia has been related to dopamine levels.

It is men who commit almost all of society's violent crimes. The antisocial personality at the root of most crimes seems to be caused by poor functioning of the left hemisphere. (The only kind of treatment that seems to control or allay these disorders is drug therapy, not psychotherapy.)

The 1970 Second International Science Study measured U.S. students' knowledge of science in grades five, nine, and twelve; and compared the results with students in 24 other nations, as well as with the performance of U.S. pupils. The differences in boys and girls were greatest in the physical sciences. For example, fifth-grade boys in all countries excelled when asked to place batteries in a flashlight correctly and to explain the reason a thrown ball returns to the ground.

Disabilities are also linked to hemispheric differences. For example, autistic, reading-disabled, and mathematically gifted children are more likely to be male, left-handed, and prone to immune disorders, including allergies. Exceptions in females are discussed in Chapter 4.

Early findings suggested that the male hormone testosterone was creating extreme cases of right-hemisphere dominance in dyslexics by somehow stunting the brain's left hemisphere. Supporting the notion was the finding reported in *The Sexual Brain* that two populations of females who received male hormones showed a similar shift toward right-hemisphere abilities. Daughters of mothers who took the drug diethylstilbestrol during pregnancy, and females who produced excess male hormones, favored visual-spatial abilities over language.

According to neuropsychologist Diane McGuinness in her book, *When Children Don't Learn: Understanding the Biology and Psychology of Learning Disabilities,* there are no real learning disabilities. What is commonly known as dyslexia (defined as reading poorly or with difficulty) is not an actual disorder. McGuinness feels that the condition of dyslexia is brought on by a society that puts too much emphasis on literacy, often imposing rules dictated by an educational system that treats all children the same regardless of their gender and individual ability. Over 75% of dyslexics are boys. By setting up two different standards, one for boys and one for girls, McGuinness calculates that overnight, 10% of all boys (representing millions of male children) would immediately be classified as normal readers for their age and sex group.

By limiting the range of accepted results, the educational system does not allow for individual talents to increase. This is especially true when it comes to reading and math skills. McGuinness argues that we are more tolerant of children's different abilities in sports and music, but not tolerant enough about their learning skills such as reading and math.

In math, there is a general belief that girls suffer from "math phobia." McGuinness observes that girls do actually fall behind the boys in mathematical ability around the seventh grade but not because of a society that wants to keep them from progressing. She points out that when the left hemisphere (male dominant) of the brain is used for the concepts of algebra and geometry, girls begin to have more difficulty.

As for hyperactivity in the classroom (90% diagnosed are boys), McGuinness suggests that a definition problem exists as to what normal behavior is for each gender. Simple annoying behavior in a male may be perceived as hyperactivity only when compared to a female of the same age group.

It becomes obvious that when we look at our educational system and how it applies to our children, we must take into account all the factors of hormones, brain hemisphere locations, genetics, diet, etc. before we can accurately assess any child's potential. In fact, our labeling of disorders may increase the child's feeling of failure, inability and low self-esteem.

CHAPTER SUMMARY

The brain is the most complex and sophisticated part of the human body.

Once the two halves of the brain could communicate with one another through the tiny bundles of nerves and fibers, consciousness emerged.

The corpus callosum is as much as 40 percent larger in women than in men.

Men predominantly use the left side of the brain, where logic, reasoning, and rational thinking take place.

Women excel at skills related to the right hemisphere of the brain, such as verbal fluency and comprehension.

Men and women may use the same sides of the brain for different purposes.

Brains (as well as bodies) are formed by sex hormones.

Structural brain differences are found in fetuses by the twenty-sixth week.

Some endorphins (chemicals produced and released in the brain) exist in men that don't exist in women, and vice versa.

It is men who commit almost all society's violent crimes.

Disabilities are linked to brain hemispheric differences.

The vast majority (75%) of those classified as dyslexics are boys.

Almost all students determined to suffer from ''math phobia'' are girls.

7

DIFFERENT MODES OF PERCEPTION

I have created a very simple model to describe our range of perception as human beings. I use it for immediate identification of behavior, much like a picture frame is used to "support" a picture. For most men and women this general model outlines a preliminary perspective of how reality might be perceived. My guess is that the percentage of the population that may fit into the androgynous category is small—less than 10%.

As the model shows, men have basically two modes of perception: physical or intellectual. Women have four modes of perception: physical, intellectual, emotional, and spiritual. These mode definitions are used to identify behavioral ranges.

I define the *physical* mode as objective reality—that which can be perceived through the five senses; hard, cold facts; or solid measurable objects. I define the *intellectual* mode as thinking, imagining, cognition, attitudes, and points of view. Later in this chapter, we'll examine the emotional and spiritual modes.

Modes of Perception

Male Modes

Physical
Intellectual

Female Modes

Physical	Intellectual
Emotional	Spiritual

THE PHYSICAL AND INTELLECTUAL MODES

A man's interaction in the world is through the physical or intellectual modes. (This description also applies to those women who use either of these two modes exclusively.) A man's orientation is perceived by his mind and expressed through his body. Men "speak" a physical language and, if educated, they "speak" a mental language. As we observed in the section on early childhood development, male babies respond to objective reality. When little boys and girls sit down with their crayons, boys draw objects and girls draw people. As intellect develops in a male, his reliance on physical expression decreases. Therefore, an "intelligent" man seeks mental solutions to problems and stress, while less educated men have to rely on physical demonstrations in order to communicate. The rational mind of an intelligent man can work against him when his allocation for resolution is passed. His mind will quickly associate any behavior as a threat in this unresolved area, and until he can intellectually (psychologically) work out the problem, he will immediately go to the physical mode of emotions. Men interpret physical reality first and immediately translate it for the mind. And the mind can resolve problems quickly if the solution is within the parameters of the intellect. A man's intelligence and the amount of time and energy he has allocated to resolve a problem will determine how quickly he turns to the physical mode for solutions. Let's keep in mind that all communications from women to men are interpreted by men through the physical and intellectual modes. A man will attempt to resolve a situation or a problem intellectually, and if he fails, he will resort to a physical solution. Men give clues and signals when they move from the intellectual to the physical mode, and they assume that women are aware of at least some of these signals.

The signals may include a focused stare, an increase in breathing rate, a rush of blood to the muscles, the mild release of adrenaline, a louder voice (barking, snarling), standing (expanding the physical image to project a mild threat), and accentuating a point with a physical gesture (pointing a finger or hitting a table top)—all demonstrations of the readiness to cross the line from the intellectual to the physical mode. This may sound a bit far-fetched, but if we observe male behavior, we'll easily note demonstrations of intellectual-to-physical transfers. "Knocking the chip off someone's shoulder" occurs when someone crosses the line from intellectual threats to a willingness to engage in physical battle. This transfer may happen instantaneously or never, depending on the intelligence of the parties involved. Behavioral modification is possible at the point where thoughts end and physical expression begins. Being able to identify this point makes it possible to modify thoughts and translate them into appropriate action or expression.

If a man is "intellectual," his emotions are in his thoughts. If his orientation is more physical, his emotions are in his body. Women experience emotions in a totally different way than men. To the man, everything is interpreted through one of his two modes of perception. Men think sad thoughts or think happy thoughts (intellect). Men express feelings through the body (physical).

It should not be surprising, therefore, that when women talk about emotions to men, men assume they mean "thinking" or "feeling." Men don't know if something is real or not until it becomes physical (objective reality). A man can plan and plan and plan, but until he actually touches the object, all his planning doesn't mean a thing to him. For example:

She says, "Wouldn't it be nice to have a new house?"

He says, "Well, you know it's a bad time of year to buy. The interest rates are up."

She says, "But isn't it a good idea?"

He says, "No, it's not a good idea because of the interest rates and [lists other facts]! When we have the money and we have the time, then we'll talk about it."

She says, "You *always* [you can fill in the rest]...."

Why does this conversation happen over and over again on a hundred different topics? What happens is that the man translates everything the woman says from the intellectual ("This is just a good idea, and I only want to talk about it") to the physical ("I am talking about a new house, and we have to do something about it right away!"). He thinks if she didn't want to do something about a new house *now,* then why would she bring it up?

When she says, "Let's just talk about this," he thinks, says, or would like to say, "Well, it's not fun for me to talk about it if it's not going to go anywhere. What's the point? The only value I see in talking with you about things that aren't going anywhere is that it's fun for you. And in order to satisfy you or please you, I will demean myself and talk about 'nonsense.' "

MOVING FROM ONE MODE TO ANOTHER

Moving from the intellectual mode to the physical mode is not necessarily negative because this is how all human beings produce physical results from ideas. In a creative way, men investigate, plan, plot, and design projects. Once the intellect has done its work, that project is then translated into the physical mode. Men do this instinctively and naturally, and they are usually unaware of making the transition from one mode to the other.

Men erroneously assume that women too, use only the intellectual and physical modes of perception. This assumption causes men to misread signals from women's emotional and spiritual modes, because men automatically translate through intellectual or physical perceptions.

THE EMOTIONAL AND SPIRITUAL MODES

The emotional and spiritual modes are not easily described by men, since they don't usually have access to these realms. I define the emotional and spiritual modes as those realms of perception that are outside and beyond objectivity, physical language, and intellectual understanding.

In describing an emotion, a man will usually point to a location in his body. He will point to his head (intellectual/spiritual), his heart (emotional/spiritual), or his stomach (emotional/physical). The way he intellectually interprets "emotion" is to remember or to imagine feelings. I suggest that women, in addition to the male experience of emotions, have a *direct experience* of emotions that is neither physical nor intellectual. This direct experience confuses the man since he assumes the woman will be and should be able to communicate her feelings through his two modes.

I'M JUST HAVING AN EMOTION

Sometimes women just *have* emotions; they are capable of experiencing emotions for no reason. Most men (and women who have been trained not to trust their own *direct* emotional and spiritual feelings) find this statement almost incomprehensible. If there is a reason for her having the emotion, the woman may not even be aware of it, but there are also times when an emotion exists purely on its own. Women sometimes "find" themselves feeling happy or sad for no reason, and they tell men so. Since men *always* have a reason for their emotions (they may not be aware of the reason, but they *know* that a reason exists), they tend to ridicule or demean a woman's emotional state, especially if she tells the man (or a male-trained woman) that there is no reason for her feeling. As a result of this great gap, women have either learned not to talk about their emotions so often, or to become adept at making up reasons for them just to pacify men. For example, if a man sees a woman looking depressed (according to his definition of depressed), the conversation might go like this:

Man: "Are you sad?"

Woman: "I guess I am."

Man: "What are you sad about?"

Woman: "I don't know."

The man (thinking he'll be helping her out of her confusion) will then try to narrow the possibilities for her sadness in order to come up with a solution for her. Men do not operate very well in conversations or circumstances that don't fit comfortably into their physical or intellectual modes. When a woman talks about something outside the man's two modes (intellectual and physical), the man assumes that she would appreciate getting out of the "I don't know" condition in the same way that he would want to be relieved of it. The woman, on the other hand, feels as if the man won't let her "be." It feels as if he is constantly picking on her or trying to make her feel unintelligent. Neither is true. He is attempting to resolve a situation which would be uncomfortable for him. He is trying to "fix" her by putting her back into the physical or intellectual modes in which he is at ease.

SPIRITUALITY

The spiritual mode is also outside man's physical and intellectual realm. Again, men have interpreted spiritualism into physical forms (icons, idols, statues, flags, dietary restrictions, elaborate cathedrals and temples) or intellectual forms (philosophy, religion, dogma, jargon, and rituals). When a religious man talks about his religion, he usually talks about its principles, structure, rituals, history, and celebrations. A woman talks of her spiritual experience. Women participate in the religious ceremony to regain an experience of spirituality.

As they do with emotions, most women perceive spirituality as a direct experience. If and when men *do* have a "spiritual" experience, they tend to organize a religion or dogma around that experience in order to fit it within their two modes. A man finds comfort in rules and regulations so that he does not have to venture into the spiritual realm very often. Those men who have attained spiritual heights on a consistent basis have given up (or never have had) control over their physical reality. Many famous male teachers and gurus have to be reminded to eat and bathe and are usually taken care of by their loyal supporters. Most men either don't have the luxury of denouncing the physical mode in order to attain that level or they don't consider the benefits worth the effort.

Women can achieve the spiritual mode without having to give up their physical reality. *Men have to choose between the physical or the spiritual* and *between the intellectual and the emotional.* One of the most frequent complaints I hear from women is that they cannot find a "balanced" male. By "balanced," women mean a man who can travel freely among the four modes as she can. Women assume that men are indulging themselves by insisting that everything be interpreted through their two modes. At the same time, men try to be patient assuming or hoping that women eventually will settle into the physical or intellectual modes before they "waste" their time trying to communicate with her.

CROSSING THE PHYSICAL BARRIER

When a man is touched, whether by a male or female, his physical barrier has been crossed. A touch is a signal that the situation has moved from the intellectual level to the physical level. This signal can be both positive (friendly gesture, sexual gesture) and/or negative (domination, territorial threat, expression of anger). Women are sometimes trained in the workplace to be careful about casual touching. What seems like simply a friendly gesture to a woman (reaching out to touch an arm or give a brief hug) might be misconstrued by a man as indicating that the relationship has moved to the physical level. If he responds according to his interpretation of his own signals by getting friendlier than the woman had intended, he's likely to feel as if he has been teased or played with, while the woman remains unaware of his feelings. Men constantly monitor such clues in all their interpersonal relationships through the intellectual or physical modes.

Competition between men is usually expressed through physical strength or intellectual endurance. Physical strength may include money, territory, or muscles as forms of physical power. Intellectual endurance includes credentials, degrees, or business/professional control as forms of intellectual power. Men are more willing to compete in the areas where they feel strongest.

DISPARITY IN PHYSICAL PLAY

When men are physically playful with women or when women try to engage in physical play with men, a number of signals are usually misinterpreted. Given a man's greater physical strength, he may feel disadvantaged and manipulated by a woman because he cannot fully release his strength with her in the same manner he could with a man. He might also assume that she is indulging in frailty, or "playing soft." As we noted earlier, a man doesn't bruise as easily as a woman, nor does he have as many nerve endings to feel pain; his skin is thicker, and his blood coagulates faster. These characteristics and attitudes can combine to overwhelm the woman, and she then translates them into apparent crudeness or a profound lack of sensitivity on the man's part. The man, knowing the disparity between his physical potential and the woman's, needs to constantly "hold back," unless the woman has a high level of testosterone or has been trained to physically compete with men. Men and women need to be aware that men have an overwhelming advantage when brute strength is a factor in competition.

EMOTIONAL DIALOGUE VERSUS ATTACK

A woman, on the other hand, cannot fully release in her emotional mode because a man is unable to withstand what *looks* like an attack on him. As with the woman's physical disadvantage, the man cannot respond emotionally at the same level as the woman. Research indicates that women generate stress just as men do, but a woman's body releases stress faster and soon returns her to "normal." The man's body is slower to return to normal, which leaves him feeling emotionally "bruised"—more so than she appears to be! A man's statement that he "can't talk or fight anymore right now" may appear that he is avoiding confrontation. But he is actually speaking the truth from his point of view. The woman is not as affected by emotions as he is, so he is inclined to protect himself from her apparent lack of concern and compassion for his reality.

Physical abuse of women by men results from the man's inability (or unwillingness) to translate his frustration into an intellectually developed emotional outlet. Physically abused women are justifiably a subject of urgent national concern, and I suggest that men and women become more knowledgeable of this subject. However, emotional abuse of men by women is rarely discussed, except in the form of jokes or derision. If a man gives feedback to a woman that she is pushing him too far, she often misinterprets his signal and thinks he is finally beginning to express emotions. Feeling that she is on the right track, she continues to push him. In my workshops women frequently say that they deliberately say things to annoy a man just to get him to open up. So in her attempt to have a man "release" through the emotional mode, a man often feels manipulated and/or severely damaged by a woman who takes advantage of her emotional "muscles."

MODE MISINTERPRETATION

Men constantly attempt to fit women's emotional states into their own interpretations of reality so that they can relate to them. Women who talk about their feelings with men can expect to be asked questions that would be useful to another man in helping him focus and identify the source of his emotion. To women, however, this interpretation takes on the qualities of narrowness and impatience on the part of the man, a dynamic to be explored later.

Unfortunately, a man's attempts to "translate" usually "cause" the woman to feel misunderstood, ignored, or "handled," and she becomes annoyed, upset, frustrated, or all of these. She then goes to a woman friend to whom she can speak. Not only were her emotional needs not met by the man; she is now disappointed because her intimate partner (whom she thought was her best friend) "let her down." Her friend's support becomes further evidence that her intimate male partner should have been able to listen to her. She now assumes that the man is the "problem." After all, her friend was able to understand and relate to her dilemma at once. A male friend may also be able to listen to her with understanding, since he is not emotionally (no energy investment) involved and can appear to be "objective" about her situation.

FIGHT OR FLIGHT

For thousands of years, men have had to make quick decisions based on "signals" received during situations that required them to take a stand (fight) or run (flight). As a result of evolution, men have built-in brain chemistry and physical attributes to naturally support the choice they make. If the response is to fight, a man's body is prepared, as we've observed, with thicker skin, fewer nerve endings, more hair, and larger lungs to supply needed oxygen to muscles. His joints are closely knit to withstand and deliver impact, his bones are thick and heavy to deflect blows, and his brain releases endorphins that trigger accelerated heartbeat. Other body chemicals further numb a man to pain (the same numbing effect produced by cocaine and morphine) and coagulate his blood faster. If the response is to run, adrenaline is released for speed, and muscles become more elastic.

THE FIVE CONCESSIONS OF WOMEN

The physical universe is the ideal male domain. The male orientation is physical, and men's brains are organized to deal with objective reality. Nevertheless, I have discovered in working with a great diversity of women's groups (and in my consulting work on a one-to-one basis) that women are constantly required to deal with a number of issues that exist only for them because *their orientation is not grounded in the physical universe.* I call these issues "concessions," and loosely describe them as unresolvable confrontations that create a sense of "giving in" or "yielding" for women.

These concessions underlie much of women's behavior, even though women may not deal with them consciously. If you are a woman, you may recognize one or all of these concessions as situations you have been tolerating or struggling with for a long, long time. Since the men around you do not seem to be having this trouble, you either blame yourself or have decided to live with what seems an almost intolerable burden. (Many gay men and extremely creative left-handed men share some, but not all, of these concessions.) If you are a man, you may recognize some of these centuries-old concessions that women have been trying to verbalize, but you may have paid them little attention.

I consider these concessions as feminine "overhead," the price women pay to live in the physical universe. But while concessions are a constant companion to women's existence in the physical universe, they do not need to be a burden.

1. Existing on the physical plane

The first concession women make is to simply exist in the physical universe. Just being in the physical universe is very confining to women. The fact that she has a body can be annoying and limiting to her. Sometimes the body gets sick and she has to take care of it, and sometimes it feels great, and sometimes it doesn't. Women have an inner sense that they don't need to be anchored or oriented in physical reality. Other realities exist for women that are not as dense as the physical universe (emotional and spiritual modes). Yet a woman must operate in objective reality, whether it's comfortable or not. She can't just snap her fingers and appear somewhere else, even though somewhere in her past experience she has a sense of being able to do just that.

I suggest that women and their relationships exist outside objective reality. What we normally call subjective reality (emotions, intuition, extra-sensory perception, spirituality, and the like) exists within the confines of the brain, but these elements are usually beyond a man's ability to perceive or understand. Men therefore demean (as most humans do) anything beyond their understanding. Is it any wonder that men relate to women as if they are unconscious, flighty, and unrealistic?

The notion that women can exist outside the male reality is very confusing to men because it implies an area beyond their control. Women continually invite men to step beyond their physical and intellectual limitations without realizing that in order for a man to maintain his sanity, he must maintain these limits. The limits are healthy for men in the same way that the limits are unhealthy for women. For men to cooperate with women, women must recognize that the physical plane (while a nuisance to her) is of crucial importance to men. Asking a man to step over the line into a woman's limitless reality may seem like a simple request to her, but to the man, it may seem life-threatening.

2. Giving up anger

Women harbor an internal anger at having been "trapped" on the physical plane. To release this anger, women must be willing to find a balance between the levels of male/female existence.

Women know that they are not as "bad" as they could be! They discipline and control a great many of their impulses and pay tremendous "overhead" to hold back their emotional anger. (The male equivalent to this concession is having to hold back physical aggression.) Sometimes women would like to create situations just to watch men squirm, but they don't. Women don't laugh as much around men as they might around other women. They stifle their spontaneity, their intelligence, and their general feminine perspective in order to get along with men.

Given all this, it is very important that women develop healthy ways to release this anger without damage to themselves or their families.

3. Giving up suppression

The third concession women make is to deal with the constant frustration of being suppressed, misunderstood, and misused. Women constantly monitor themselves in order to be "appropriate," but since they are usually judged according to male reality, there seems to be no way to consistently be "okay." Women must define their own reality and develop self-esteem that is not based on male standards.

4. Holding the male reality

The fourth concession women make is having to hold the male notion of reality. Women have to be able to work in the rational, physical world in order to get along with men, but men don't have to be able to live in the feminine world to survive. Women constantly compromise to keep the peace. (Men compromise also to avoid conflict.) Sometimes women will agree with men just so men will "back off." If women back off, they are accused of being submissive; if they stand and fight, they are accused of being a bitch, even as they watch their energy being misused. Until men are aware of and respect the female reality, both men and women are in a no-win situation.

5. Patience

The fifth concession women make is to be patient until men's dependence on the physical plane is transformed so that we as a species can move toward including the intuitive and the spiritual realms with less dependency on physical reality.

These concessions make sense to women. Yet most men don't realize the hardships women experience when operating within the confines of a physical universe, nor the enormous implications of these concessions.

When men can't explain something, they relegate it to the outer limits of the unknown, or to spirituality, or to a matter of luck, whether good or bad. And while men may complain about the physical objective reality, they find comfort in its predictability.

There has always been a battle of the sexes. However, 15,000 years ago, the battle of the sexes was a topic of discussion only among the wealthy, or was portrayed through mythological powers and deities in male and female form. With an average life span of twenty-four years, most of the population was busy just surviving, and most human beings weren't aware of the battle, much less its intensity. In many societies, men and women now have enough leisure time to find out that we're not compatible, and I suggest that it's only very recently we've discovered the immensity of our differences.

As humans, we seem to develop through individual potential and environmental necessity. This interplay (nature and nurture) seems to govern our genetic evolvement, but leaves us at the mercy of ourselves.

Many people consider the feminine qualities of caring and connectedness to be immature and unnecessary, though in my opinion it was and is one of the most important elements in the development of civilization. Surely the time has come to redefine what it means to be a mature adult and to incorporate feminine values into the new emerging model of a "balanced humanity."

If we employ our ability to manage our thinking and alter the way in which we live, we can create some options. But these options will still be expressed through the bodies in which we live. For that reason, it's about time we became both familiar and at ease with our differences.

Behavioral Ranges

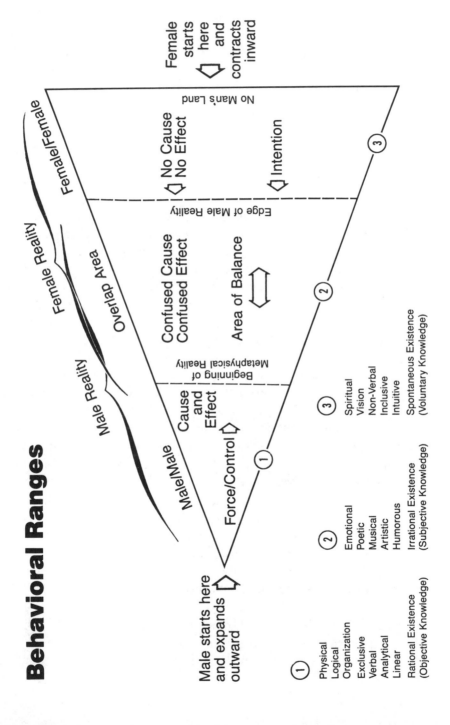

Male starts here and expands outward

Female starts here and contracts inward

Female/Female

Female Reality

Overlap Area

Male Reality

Male/Male

No Man's Land

No Cause No Effect

Intention

Edge of Male Reality

Confused Cause Confused Effect

Area of Balance

Beginning of Metaphysical Reality

Cause and Effect

Force/Control

① Physical
Logical
Organization
Exclusive
Verbal
Analytical
Linear

Rational Existence
(Objective Knowledge)

② Emotional
Poetic
Musical
Artistic
Humorous

Irrational Existence
(Subjective Knowledge)

③ Spiritual
Vision
Non-Verbal
Inclusive
Intuitive

Spontaneous Existence
(Voluntary Knowledge)

At the beginning of this chapter I stated that modes of perception are manifested as behavior ranges. The behavioral-range model elaborates my theories about male and female realities and how they are perceived. You may be able to locate yourself and others in the model and begin to see why and where your relationship issues may be in conflict.

CHAPTER SUMMARY

Men have basically two modes of perception: physical and intellectual.

Women have four modes of perception: physical, intellectual, emotional, and spiritual.

A man's orientation is perceived by his mind and expressed through his body.

"Intelligent" men seek mental solutions to problems and stress.

Less intelligent men rely on physical demonstrations in order to communicate.

Men give clues and signals when going from the intellectual to the physical mode.

Men do not know if something is real or not until it becomes physical (objective reality).

Men erroneously assume that women use only the intellectual and physical modes of perception.

Moving from the intellectual mode to the physical mode is a positive step in producing physical results from ideas.

Women have a direct experience of emotions and spirituality that is neither physical nor intellectual.

Men have interpreted spiritualism in physical or intellectual forms.

When a man is touched, whether by a male or female, his perception is placed in the physical mode.

Competition between men is usually expressed through physical strength or intellectual endurance.

Men have an advantage over women when brute strength is a factor in competition.

Men often feel manipulated and/or damaged by any woman who takes advantage of her emotional "muscles."

A woman generates stress just as a man does, but her body releases
stress faster and returns her to "normal" more quickly.

Men have built-in brain chemistry and physical attributes to naturally
support the choice between "fight" or "flight."

Women constantly make a number of concessions because their
perceptual orientation is not grounded in the physical universe.

Concessions are unresolvable confrontations which create a sense of
"giving in" or "yielding" for women.

Five concessions women make:
    Existing on the physical plane
    Giving up anger
    Giving up suppression
    Maintaining "male" reality
    Patience

As humans, we seem to develop through individual potential and
environmental necessity.

8

OBJECTIVE VERSUS SUBJECTIVE REALITY

Understanding some of the limitations and options that exist for us as human beings can relieve the pressure that comes from thinking that there may be something wrong with us and can give us an appreciation for the "natural" behavior of others, even though it may be different than our own.

UNTRANSLATABLE DIFFERENCES

We've all observed that even though men and women are of the same species, there are experiences in life that are unique to males and females. Men will never know what it is like to carry a baby for nine months or have a menstrual cycle. (Even among women, the experience may vary, but the commonality of the experience is understood and shared.) The woman can attempt to describe the experience to the man in what she considers "equivalent" terms, but it will never be fully translatable. A man can only guess about the sensations of carrying life inside his body, or the effects on a woman of her heightened sensitivity to sound, temperature, and touch.

Similarly, men's experiences of life are not always translatable to women. For instance, men often react to situations because of gender programming from the past.

Men's bodies and minds evolved to support the function of hunter. They have the ability to judge time and distance because their lives depended on it. They needed to know exactly how far away an animal or an enemy was; they needed to know how fast to run or how far a rival could throw a spear. These mechanical skills were developed over hundreds of thousands of years.

An example of this instinctual behavior in today's world is the man and his date, talking and having a good time at dinner in a restaurant. Then they go out into the dark parking lot, and you can watch the man, who had been relaxed and amiable in the restaurant, clam up and become very quiet. What he is doing on an unconscious level is scanning to see if there is any danger in the parking lot. He not only has to protect himself, but he also has to protect the woman. There are chemicals being released in his body. There are endorphins being released in his brain as if there is a potential physical threat. He is scanning with his radar system, and she, oblivious, wants to keep talking.

She says, "Oh, wasn't that fun? What do you want to do now?"

His jaw starts to clench, and by the time they reach the car, he's annoyed, and she has no idea why. (He may not know either!) The reason he is annoyed is because he's hurt and angry that she's been so inconsiderate. There he was, trying to save her life (it doesn't matter that there was no real threat—the environment and the particular circumstances make him feel and respond as if he is actually susceptible to attack), and all she is doing is "jabbering" about something that isn't important or significant to him. He thinks: "It could have waited until we were safe and secure in the car." And feels uneasy with her.

Most men are not even conscious that this process goes on. When I use this example in my workshops, men say, "Oh, I didn't realize that's what was happening. But you're right. I do that," or "I thought she *knew* what I was doing."

EGO ORIENTATION

One of the evolutionary results of specialization in the male brain is his orientation or point of view—how he perceives his place on the planet. The word normally used for this orientation is ego. The first dictionary definition of ego is simply: "The self; the individual as aware of himself."

In the way that I am using it to describe male reality, ego is a word that women will never, never experientially understand. Outside its use in clinical psychology, the word is most often used in a negative connotation, and its implications include self-righteousness, inconsideration, and conceit.

A major distinction between men and women is this focal point or "ego" orientation.

The Misunderstood Male Ego

A man's reality starts inside himself and moves outward. He begins with a "spot" inside his body. (If he is intellectual, his "spot" is in his head; if he is physical, the spot is usually located in his heart or stomach.) He expands outwardly, expending energy, and begins to interact with the physical universe through what is normally defined as "consciousness." This means that he is now aware of more than just his "spot"; he's now conscious of his body. As he continues to move outward, he becomes conscious of his environment and the things around him. (Each time he moves further "out," it costs him energy.) Everything around him is now in relation to his spot and relative to his spot. His spot is the center of his universe. He has to be the center of his universe because everything revolves around him. A man's orientation is exclusive, discriminatory, and analytical.

When a man walks into a room, he finds a place where his "spot" will be comfortable. Then he starts to move outward. If he has enough energy, he will continue to expand until he finally includes the entire room. It costs him energy to stay "out," and the amount of energy expended depends on how strong he is, how smart he is, and how much control he can maintain of his surroundings. (If he gets tired, observe how he moves inward until all he can deal with is himself. He doesn't have energy for anything else.)

If you want to test a man's "consciousness," have him close his eyes and then ask, "How many lights are in the room? How big is the room? How many square feet are there?" He will have analyzed all of that (or other factors of importance) in order for him to understand where he is in the physical universe.

Men are Exclusive

On the basis of how men's brains are organized, I suggest that men's natural orientation is "exclusive," as defined by Webster:

1. Excluding all others; shutting out other considerations, happenings, existences, occupations, (i.e.; as vegetable and mineral are exclusive terms);
2. Having the tendency or power to exclude all others;
3. Excluding all but what is specified.

To further clarify "exclusive" in this context, it is important to remember that men discriminate through objective reality (time, distance, and measurement). By having a single location or a specific starting point, all reality can be established.

Men locate themselves in the center of their existence and use up energy (stored fat, money, trade items, or personality) as they expand beyond the "spot" to interact with the physical universe.

One of the measurements of a man is his sphere of influence. Remember, men measure everything: territory, companies, houses, bank accounts—everything! A very "conscious" man is someone who can stay outside himself longer than someone else. From his center, his strength is measured by how much of the world around him he can affect or control. His "power" may be energy in the form of physical stamina (some men are good leaders simply because they can outlast others), or money (he can buy the stamina of others), or personality (he can convince others to contribute their power).

A strong-willed man expends large amounts of energy to maintain control of those elements over which he possesses exclusive rights. He will retreat to his "spot" occasionally to "refuel" (or re-energize), but he never informs anyone when he is doing so. This recovery period for him is a moment of vulnerability. He must "recharge" and regain control before anyone notices his energy depletion. Some men have limited influence and can control only their immediate environment or circumstances, such as their jobs or where they live. If a man is somehow disempowered, his ability to expand and affect his environment is diminished, as is his sense of "self." His power base is small, and his influence reflects that. If a man cannot control his environment, his frustration and anger may be turned against family or co-workers.

Most women don't have this "exclusive" orientation, and if a man says, "I am the center of the universe," it sounds as if he is saying, "I am the center of the universe, *and you're not.*" It seems very self-centered if the man says, "Everything revolves around me." But it is not an egotistical statement; it's true for him, and men interact with each other this way. It is not intended as an insult, nor is it demeaning, because men assume the same orientation of each other. A man relates to the things around him, and then responds to them. He knows *what* he is doing by where his "spot" is. And where he is standing or sitting is his "spot"; he is emanating from that location, and everything outside of him is part of his universe. If he is in a room, it is "his" room, "his" chairs, "his" tables, and "his" pen. When something in the room is moved, the man will have to refocus his attention by returning to his internal "spot" for a moment. He will then begin the process of expending energy to reorient who he is by what is happening around him in physical reality. He is now newly defined, because the elements in his universe have been redefined. To the extent that he can control the elements in his universe (keep them from indiscriminately moving about), he can manage how much energy he expends to be alive. A man uses less and less energy if things stay the same.

Once the man has defined his "spot" within the room, the walls restrict outside interference, and he does not need to expend energy to deal with anything outside the walls. Being in an enclosed space (rules and regulations act as "walls") is comforting for the man because he has fixed objects to deal with. If a wall disappears, he has to include new elements into his environment, thereby expending more energy. To the extent that there are four walls (a relatively permanent limitation), he need only expend enough energy to fill the room. He can then relax.

If furniture in a man's room is rearranged without his knowledge, he will be confused for a moment. He may not be immediately aware of the difference, but he knows that something is not as he expected it to be. One can actually observe this confusion until the change is identified (this may be a conscious or unconscious search on his part). He will return to his internal "spot," expend energy to find out what has been changed and where it now is, adjust, and then be comfortable again. This process may take seconds or months, depending on his energy and his level of self-esteem. (These factors also determine how quickly he becomes disoriented.)

If something is changed in his room without his "permission," he's likely to be confused, frustrated, and angry. In his reality, he is now forced to shift who and where he is in the universe. If someone other than himself causes this shift, he has two choices: He can try to control whoever or whatever is causing the change outside himself or he can submit by trying to avoid the source or recurrence of the change. He will attempt to manage his physical environment so that it doesn't control him and make him reorient constantly. He will attempt to set up rules so that changes will be regulated, or so he can vent his anger and frustration on the rule breaker.

Some Consequences of Men's Exclusivity

A typical example of how problems arise in a relationship as a result of men's exclusive reality is the scene of a man watching a television program. It may not be a significant program; it could be a rerun, or even a commercial. *The point is that the television has his attention.* A newspaper, book, or hobby could also be used in this example.

The woman approaches the man, whose full attention is on the television, and begins to talk. (Actually, he's *in* the television, but this is alien to most women's understanding.) The man begins to feel an intrusion, a kind of buzzing feeling or just a sound coming from somewhere. He is not sure where this feeling is coming from yet, but he is hoping it will go away. The woman continues to talk as if she were talking to another woman, who, like her, can focus on more than one thing at a time. Realizing that the intrusion is not going to go away, the man takes his attention from the television and with a mildly annoyed look on his face and a slight edge in his voice says, "Huh?"

She says, "So what do you think?"

He says, "What do I think about what?" (His annoyance mounts.)

She says, "What I've been talking about!" (By now, she's sure she's dealing with a case of brain damage.)

He says, "I didn't hear what you said!"

The woman now finds herself with one or all of the following alternatives:

1. She can take a deep breath and repeat herself from the beginning. She is tolerating the man and believes that either he doesn't care about anything but himself, or she submits to his annoyance and believes that maybe there is something wrong with her because he has treated her as not worthy of his full attention.
2. She can assume that he really heard her but is pretending to avoid the issue and repeat, "So, what do you think?" He becomes frustrated with her repetition because it appears she doesn't or won't believe that he didn't hear her.
3. She has answered her own question in the meantime and can respond with, "Oh, that's okay. Never mind."

He says, "Never mind? Never mind! You interrupted me for a never mind?"

The woman does not realize that she was an intrusion to the man, and he doesn't realize that she would not have been an intrusion to another woman (or a woman-trained male.)

His "spot" became his focus on the television, and it required energy expenditure for him to come out of the television, bring his attention back to himself, and then focus his attention on the source of the interruption. He is not upset with her in particular, however. Any interruption—the dog, the kids, a phone call, a noise outside—would cause the same reaction. The woman is simply another object to be dealt with in his objective reality. The woman's reality, in terms of relationship and partnership, allows her to interact with many "objects" simultaneously without any one of them creating a particular problem.

Unfortunately, both the man and the woman in this example think the other person is being inconsiderate, which is not true. What is true is that both are making an assumption that they operate from the same reality.

A man assumes that every human being has the same orientation to the physical universe. Most men aren't aware of this concept on a conscious level, but if a man observes his experience as a man, he will discover his "spot" orientation in the universe. Where he is physically located is his ego. He identifies who he is by knowing the things around him, and *everything outside him defines and reflects on him and his spot.* When he has identified, located, and can control as many things as necessary in his environment, he can be at ease.

Women are Inclusive

Women are contextual. They have no one fixed "spot," but are holistic in their approach to reality. Perceptually, women exist outside physical reality, and to men they appear to be present on the fringes of their (male, physical) reality.

Most women have to contract (limit) their awareness to relate to physical reality. A woman has to leave the limitless freedom of her reality to become focused and single-minded. Women expend energy to enter into and interact with physical reality. When women want to recover or reserve energy, they escape physical limitations by movement, imagination, or interaction with others. They are inclusive.

"Inclusive" as defined by Webster:

1. Including or tending to include; especially taking everything into account; reckoning everything;
2. Including the terms, limits or extremes mentioned.

That one of the definitions of "inclusive" is "including...the extremes" means that women see a picture *beyond* the limitations in order to see the limitations. Men go as far as the limitations will allow, but not beyond.

Being "exclusive" or "inclusive" are demonstrations of how men and women perceive reality. It's easy to see how and why we get ourselves into trouble by assuming that the other gender is operating with the same orientation.

Being inclusive, women do not usually break down time and distance, nor are they as concerned with "energy leaks" as men. Participants in the workshops often observe that women tend to leave lights on, or the television and radio playing when they are not in a room. In one workshop, a man related his story of how he fixed the "light" problem: He said proudly, "I've fixed that problem of her leaving the lights on in the closet."

"How did you do that?" all the men eagerly asked.

"Well, I simply put one of those switches on the door, so that when she closes the door, the light automatically goes off!"

All the men laughed and thought that was a great idea.

"How do you get her to close the door?" I asked.

He said, "I'm working on it!"

Women and Context

Women start from the place on the Reality Model labeled "Inclusive Reality" (context, outside physical reality) and move inwardly toward their "spot," never actually being able to reach it. Women's common experience of walking into a room—any room—is that in order to fit in the room, she has to get smaller. Women have to shut off the part of their non-physical experience that is outside the room. Women experience themselves as bigger than the room, and when they enter, it actually limits them. They feel manipulated, suppressed, and controlled by walls, because the walls stop women from having the experience that exists outside the room. (This is not necessarily a conscious feeling for all women, but when this scenario is discussed in women's workshops, all the women nod in recognition.) After discussing the concepts of inclusive and exclusive with women in a corporate workshop, a woman manager returned to the next session with a fine example. She had conducted a staff meeting where both men and women were present, and without warning, she had asked everyone in the staff meeting to close their eyes. She had then asked the male and female staff members to describe the room. *All* of the men were able to define the size of the room, the number of chairs, the distances from the walls, and the number of men and women present. Not one of the women could describe the details of the room as accurately as the men (some women were not sure of the number of walls, partitions, or windows), but the women were much more aware than the men of the conversation going on at the time they were asked to close their eyes, the feelings in the room, the attitudes of each individual, the temperature, and the color scheme of the room.

Male and Female Reality Model

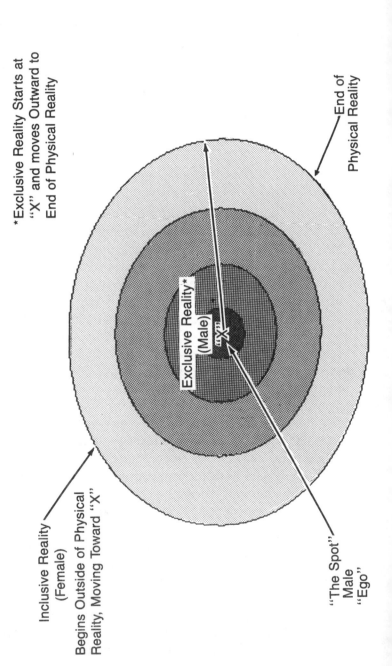

*Exclusive Reality Starts at "X" and moves Outward to End of Physical Reality

Exclusive Reality* (Male) "X"

End of Physical Reality

Inclusive Reality (Female) Begins Outside of Physical Reality, Moving Toward "X"

"The Spot" Male "Ego"

This manager's example is also an excellent demonstration of how gender differences are sometimes used against an individual to prove that he or she was *not paying attention.* To a man, paying attention means knowing the physical information in the room. To a woman, paying attention (being aware) means being sensitive to the subjective environment (the senses, the emotional relationships in the room). Men use women's lack of attention to physical detail as proof that they are not as "intelligent" or "conscious" as men, and therefore not as reliable. Women use men's lack of attention to the subjective environment as proof that men are inconsiderate of others, insensitive to what is *really* going on, and therefore not as compassionate or as loving as women are.

It appears to men as if women are deliberately behaving in ways that always keep men on edge. When men apply male standards or modes of behavior to women, they appear scattered, flighty, and disrespectful of men's physical reality. When women apply female standards to men, they appear stubborn, inflexible, and humorless. It is impossible for two people to work harmoniously or to maintain a loving relationship if both parties are waiting for the other person to change, especially when those changes make no sense to the respective parties expected to undergo them!

CHAPTER SUMMARY

There are experiences in life that are unique to males and females.

Men and women often react to situations because of gender programming from the past.

A major distinction between men and women is "ego" orientation.

A man's reality starts with his "spot" and moves outward.

Moving away from the "spot" costs the man energy.

A man's orientation is exclusive, discriminatory, and analytical.

One of the measurements a man uses is his sphere of influence.

Men retreat to their "spot" to refuel, re-energize, or to regain control.

A man is at the center of his universe and everything relates to him.

A man uses less and less energy when things stay the same.

A woman's reality allows her to simultaneously interact with many "objects."

Women are inclusive and holistic in their approach to reality.

Women can exist outside physical reality and appear to men to be on the fringes of male (physical) reality.

Women have to contract their awareness to relate to physical reality.

Women expend energy to enter into and interact with physical reality.

Women see a picture *beyond* the limitations in order to see the limitations.

Women generally feel manipulated, suppressed, and controlled by walls.

Men generally experience a sense of freedom within limitations such as walls or rules.

9

ALLOCATION OF ENERGY

Another area of likely misinterpretation between males and females relates to a concept I call "allocation of energy." A man unconsciously monitors the energy he expends from his fat reserves because if they become depleted, he literally runs out of energy. He doesn't have the endurance of a woman. (Refer to Chapter 5.) A man allocates a certain amount of time to do a task; then he stops. He expends his energy and then has to "go inside" himself to recover.

Men recover energy in one of two ways:

1. They "go back into their bodies," which usually takes the form of naps or long periods of sleep; or
2. They focus on one particular thing, such as television or a book.

During the recovery period, men overtly or covertly give out the message, "Don't bother me! I've just used up my energy, and I have to go back inside to restore myself." (Women may also need to withdraw under unusual stress. Generally, however, they are capable of recovering energy while continuing to interact with the outside world.)

Here is another clear example that when we assume men and women are the same, we set up unrealistic expectations about feelings or behavior. If a male has been working on a project side-by-side with a woman, he has consciously or unconsciously allocated a specific amount of energy, and he needs to know where the beginning, middle, and end of the project is likely to be. This is, again, a situation that truly frustrates women: "Why do men always need to know the end? Why can't we just process, just discover, just play, and then find out where it all goes?"

It's not easy for a man to be spontaneous, because he needs to know in advance when he will run out of energy. A woman's metabolism and fat system make her energy different than his. She has a fat reserve that he doesn't have. She can simply take a breath and say "Okay, let's go," and then proceed to the next task. Because a man can't do that as easily, he is very concerned (and probably doesn't know why) that his energy may be misused. To the woman, it looks as if the man is being inflexible, stubborn, or even may be eating the wrong foods. (Women know that if men just ate better, they would have more energy. And the truth is that men definitely *could* eat better; they devote much less attention to balanced meals and nutrition than women.)

A woman expends and depletes energy in order to get focused. Job stress occurs for women when the boss says, "Here are some details; keep your attention on this." Most women have to restrict themselves uncomfortably (compared to men) in order to stay focused for long periods of time. Then, when they're through "focusing," they need to get back *outside* themselves to recover. They want to go for walks, see a movie, or engage in other forms of play. They want to talk, they want to express, they want to do something to get out of that narrow little box that costs them such huge amounts of energy. This is exactly the opposite of a man's need to "go inside" after working "outside" himself.

What typically happens in a household at the end of a day? The man comes home and wants to relax, watch television, fall asleep, or do nothing. The woman might suggest that they go out to eat. The man will probably say something like, "Why didn't you tell me this morning you wanted to go out tonight?" Since the woman does not have to be as concerned about her supply of energy, she does not have to be as careful as a man in planning its expenditure.

Even if she manages to "nag" him into submission, he still needs recovery time. So he says, "Just give me twenty minutes, honey, and I'll be fine. Leave me alone."

She says, "Okay, I'll leave you alone. How are you feeling?"

(What men mean by "leave me alone" is, "I need to get back in my head" or "my body," depending on which mode he is in.)

If the woman is unable to relate to his needs, she might say, "Just let me sit next to you. I won't bother you." Or she might say, "Why can't we talk while you're relaxing?" She doesn't realize that activity of any kind costs the man attention energy. A man has to leave his "spot" even to talk, or he has to come out of himself to deal with her touch. Women have the ability to mentally "check in" and "check out" at will. When it gets a little hot in a room, or if it gets a little boring, they just leave. Their bodies stay, but their energy leaves. Actually, the woman goes somewhere else in her experience, probably to re-energize enough to tolerate the room until she can escape from its confines. When women do this, men think they're being flighty or that they can't pay attention. "What's wrong with them? Why can't they just stay focused?" Men want women to be focused in order to determine if they're conscious and whether or not they can be trusted. Men also demean other men if they don't pass the "consciousness" test.

One of the first things a student of assertive communication learns is to get the other person's full attention. The supposition is, if you don't have the person's full attention, they're telling you in a very subtle way that you don't matter. Since men can only focus on one thing at a time, focus is an important issue in male communication. If a man walks into a woman's office and she's answering the phone or writing memos, he "knows" he is being demeaned. (He assumes he is not as important to her as the phone call or memo.) Women, on the other hand, can do five, six, or ten things at once. If a woman says, "You have my full attention," and continues to work on something, a man is likely to say, "No, look at my face. Look at me when I'm talking!" He can't believe she can successfully be doing two things at once. (See Chapter 6.)

One of my female workshop participants gained some insight on male focus during an incident that she described to us:

> I was watching the Super Bowl on television with the guys one afternoon, and while I was watching, I was also working on the checkbook, making some lists, knitting or sewing, or something

else. All the men turned to me and said, "Either watch the game or get the hell out!"

To the men, it appeared that if she were really interested in the game, she couldn't possibly be doing anything else—because men couldn't. They assumed that she was intentionally demeaning their reality. They also assumed that she was flighty and couldn't really have meant it when she said that she was actually paying attention.

Men also can't understand how women can leave the theater or the living room during the most important part of a movie and go to the bathroom. A man will hold it! He has his priorities. He also has a larger bladder! On the other hand, the woman's "inclusive" mode gives her a sense of what's going on in the film, and she can still "watch" the film while she's in the bathroom. If the man is not physically watching the movie, he misses out. Even though she may not have caught all the details, she doesn't have a sense of missing anything.

WHO'S WORKING HARDER?

Let's assume that a man and woman are working side-by-side on a task or project. She's giving 100%, and the man is giving 100%; but when the task is completed, the man is *done,* expended, and must return to his "spot." He determines what task is next, checks his energy reserves, and prepares for a rest and recovery period. But the woman is likely to behave in quite a different way. Not only is she more energetic than the man at the end of the task, but throughout she was probably more talkative and mobile than he. To add insult to injury, she probably did more than just the task at hand, as in the football example, and when the task was complete, she was ready to have some fun or to go directly on to the next project. The man then makes an unconscious automatic assumption that the woman didn't work as hard as he did. After all, he knows that if she had, she would be just as tired as he is.

The man therefore devalues the woman's work, based on his mistaken assumptions. He *had* to stay focused on the task before him, and the woman's relative lack of attention (according to his standard) has confused him in his attempt to understand how she approached the task.

Men and women might enjoy working together more if we could work with the same set of "tools" or if we understood how our different approaches to a task compliment each other.

THE MISUSE OF ENERGY

The couch move is a classic disagreement between men and women. This is one of my favorite examples of inclusive/exclusive reality, allocation of energy, and control. Whenever I use this example in the workshops, both the men and women groan in recognition.

First of all, men ask, *"Why* move the couch?" Since men have to monitor their allocation of energy, they first must be able to relate to the *need* for the couch to be moved. If the man is not convinced and moves it anyway, he has misused his energy, a fact that sheds considerable light on the male credo of "If it's not broken, don't fix it!"

So the woman innocently wanders into the male reality and asks the man to help her move the couch. He says, "Sure, no problem." He loves her, so he grits his teeth, takes some energy away from his reserves, looks at where the couch is going, mentally envisions moving it, and then physically moves the couch. Beginning, middle, and end. He has done the task for which he has allocated energy. Then she says, "I don't like it under the window; let's try it against the wall over there."

The man begins to get angry. Nevertheless, if he's in relatively good shape (not overly stressed or low on energy), he takes a breath, readjusts his universe, and allocates some *more* energy (he had only allocated enough for one move) to help her take the couch where she wants it.

Then she might say, "I liked it where it was before/It really doesn't fit/We need a new couch/Let's try the table now."

He snarls, "When you know where you want the – – – couch, let me know." Or "Where's the graph paper? Why didn't you measure it first?"

Men become frustrated with constant moving because they know they expend less energy in mental activity than they do in physical motion. A man probably would have measured the room, the wall, and the couch; he would have located electrical outlets and measured the lamp cords, so that he would only have had to move the couch once.

There's no question in his mind that the woman has been inconsiderate, selfish, and demeaning. She has just misused his energy. If she really cared about him, she would have thought it through (intellectual) before asking for his help (physical).

When I observe women moving objects or hanging pictures with other women, it appears that the more they move, the more fun they seem to be having. (And they laugh and make jokes while they're doing it!) Men certainly don't laugh and make jokes while they're moving something! Because every time a man moves something, he has to go back inside himself, reallocate his energy, reorient, and then come back out. Laughing and having a good time would use up some of the energy he allocated for the move.

Women are not fixated by physical items the way men are. The relocation of the couch was not a problem to the woman because everything in her environment is part of her experience. She was having fun; there was movement in her physical world. Yet movement alters a man's entire orientation.

A man arranges his apartment the way he wants it and could keep it that way for twenty years. Why bother moving something when it works? To a woman, this implies that things are fixed, stagnating, uncreative, not evolving. She feels limited by a permanent physical arrangement because her world is not fixed; it's mobile and moving all the time. A man's world *is* fixed.

Part of the sense of freedom that women want (the sense of spontaneity, the sense of joy at being alive) is supplied by having things lively, animate, moving around. So the more men attempt to put structure in a woman's life, the more she feels dominated, manipulated, oppressed, angry, and misunderstood.

MONITORING MUSCLE POWER

As we noted in Chapter 5, men need to monitor energy on a subconscious level for a number of reasons. Their striated muscles (more fibrous, and therefore bulkier and more defined) use energy in a less efficient manner than women's. Striated muscles allow imme-

Non-Focus

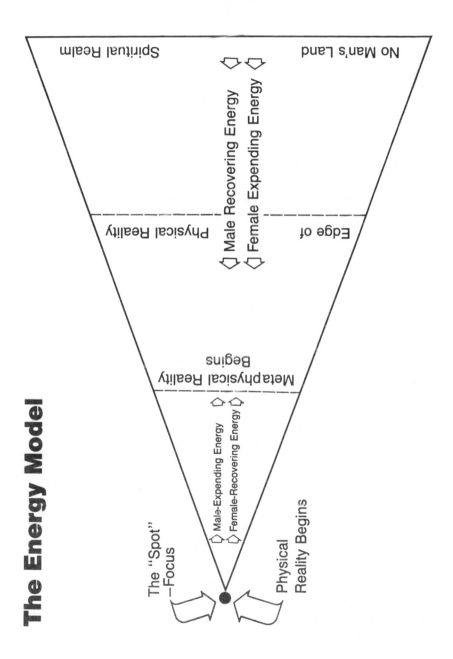

The Energy Model

No Man's Land — Spiritual Realm

Male Recovering Energy
Female Expending Energy

Edge of — Physical Reality

Metaphysical Reality Begins

Male-Expending Energy
Female-Recovering Energy

The "Spot" —Focus

Physical Reality Begins

diate use of strength, but burn energy (that is, generate more heat) faster, thereby depleting the body's reserves more quickly.

Men and women not only store body fat differently, they also store different types of glucose and gain access to it differently. Men produce endorphins to handle immediate stress, but they wear down faster than women do in prolonged stressful situations.

THE UPSET OF CHANGE

In my workshops, women usually complain about men's unwillingness to change. Most men are reluctant about change. Now you can understand why women think men are being stubborn. Men think women change too much, and that if the man didn't "drag his feet," he would be in the constant danger and confusion that change can mean to him. However, change is not always disturbing to men, especially if they are the instigators. If a man initiates a change, he has already calculated and allocated the necessary energy to make the change. He is in control. If someone else instigates the change, he has to determine if it's necessary, and if he decides or allows that it is, he will allocate his energy accordingly. In the single matter of energy allocation alone lies a reassuring explanation for us about what puts the sexes at odds with one another so often. Staying aware of it and our other differences can go a long way toward resolving what so often exasperates us into our own version of Dagwood and Blondie or other less benign characters.

CHAPTER SUMMARY

Men consciously or unconsciously allocate and monitor expenditures of energy from the body's fat reserves.

Women have fat reserves that men don't have, and the female metabolism and fat system regulates energy expenditure/recovery in a very different way.

Men recover energy by going back into their bodies or by focusing on one particular thing.

Women are capable of recovering energy while continuing to interact with the outside world.

Men need to be able to identify beginning, middle, and end as part of the allocation of energy process.

Men are not naturally spontaneous.

Women need to return outside themselves to recover energy, a process that is exactly opposite of men's need to go inside.

Women do not have to be as concerned as men about energy supply, nor as careful about its expenditure.

Women have the ability to mentally "check in" and "check out" at will; their bodies stay, but their energy leaves.

Men want women to be focused in order to determine if they're conscious and whether or not they can be trusted.

Men can only focus on one thing at a time, and focus is an important function in male communication.

Women can focus on many things at once.

Men sometimes devalue the work of women based on mistaken assumptions about work styles.

Most men live by "If it's not broken, don't fix it!"

Men expend less energy in mental activity than in physical motion.

Everything in a woman's environment is part of her experience.

Women feel limited by permanent physical arrangements because their world is mobile and moving all the time.

The imposition of structure makes most women feel dominated, manipulated, oppressed, angry, and misunderstood.

Men can handle immediate stress, but they wear down more quickly than women in prolonged stressful situations.

If a man initiates a change, he has already calculated and allocated the energy necessary to make the change.

10

MAKING IT HAPPEN VERSUS LETTING IT HAPPEN

SEQUENTIAL / ASEQUENTIAL THINKING

Women approach problems with an overview (using both hemispheres of the brain simultaneously), while men need and tend to segregate problems into component parts in order to arrive at a solution.

Women "see" holistically and men "see" on a highly linear basis. Men use logic to determine trust, because facts build trust. For men, facts lead to logical conclusions ("a," therefore "b," therefore "c," therefore "d"); and if the sequence is broken, all future conclusions or decisions are suspect. Men use sequence to build points in arguments, and they become frustrated when women seem to bypass what to them is unarguably "reality."

What traditionally happens in business meetings when a problem arises is that men operate sequentially—a, b, c, d—as they develop their logic system to reach a solution or conclusion. These sequential patterns are important to men and allow them to trust the "proof." Women, however, can look at the whole picture, pick out something asequentially—a, c, d, b,—and say, "Oh, I know what we should do." But a man can't trust her "non-process."

Example: A woman gives a solution to a problem five minutes after the meeting begins. Her solution is accurate, but the men can't hear it because they're not ready for it. They haven't been through the "a, b, c, d" steps yet. The men will talk and argue; then an hour later, a man will give the exact same solution as the woman's. All the men will say, "Yes, that's dead on; that's what we should do." The woman has no alternative but to think that men simply don't listen to her because she is a woman. The fact is, the men didn't listen to her not because the information was being offered by a woman, but because they were not *ready* for the information. If a man had made the same suggestion out of sequence, it would also have been ignored.

If the woman had written her suggestion on the chalkboard during the discussion, she could then have pointed to it (with as little smugness as possible, I would hope) so that the men could give her credit for her idea. Otherwise, the men will recall a different version of her original solution; that is, if and when she asks for credit.

It is important for a woman to document her work and make sure she gets credit for it. This behavior may seem separative and unlike a team player to women, but it is what male members of the team would do, and they would expect her to do the same. They believe that if she doesn't value her work very highly, they shouldn't either.

Here's another example of sequential/asequential thinking:

He says, "Do you know where the restaurant is?"

She says, "Sure, I've been there for lunch."

Depending on the condition of the relationship, the man may ask for specific proof that the woman knows its location (which may result in a fight), or he can avoid the question and wait for her to make a mistake on the way (clenching his jaw, pretending to be calm). The woman may have been "trained" to be a good "navigator" in order to avoid the problem. Yet if she hasn't been male-trained, or doesn't think it's important to "be prepared" or forgets herself for a moment and acts naturally, she might say out loud: "I wonder. Is it this turn or the next?"

The man immediately assumes that she has no idea where she is going, and that she lied when she said she knew how to get there. In his system, since she didn't know what to do at stage "b," she obviously won't know about "c," or "d" either. Things can only get worse. His conclusion: She is out of control!

When the woman said she knew how to get to the restaurant, she simply envisioned herself there. Even if they get lost, what's the big deal? She knows it will all work out, and she trusts the process. Besides, rediscovering how to get there could be fun; an adventure! She might even spot a more promising, livelier restaurant on the way. (However, she shouldn't expect the man to be thrilled if she suggests a change in restaurants for he has to reorient and answer multiple questions that arise for him in that case, such as, "Do they take credit cards? What's on the menu? Am I dressed appropriately? Is the service decent?")

Because of their process of allocating energy and their sequential thinking, men are not as flexible as women about changing plans. By developing systems that can be repeated over and over again with the least number of failures and the least amount of energy expenditure, life (for a man) runs very smoothly. While a man's ability to be sequential is admired (men are very willing to do routine tasks without question once the reason and reward have been established), I've observed that his lack of spontaneity is usually a point of frustration for women. (Every positive quality has a "negative" side to it!)

Another example of sequential thinking was presented by a married couple in the workshop. The woman had complained to her husband that he never did the grocery shopping. He told her he would be happy to buy groceries if she would help him get organized. She agreed, but didn't realize what she was agreeing to! A few days later, he returned to her with a careful diagram of the grocery store. Each aisle was clearly marked, as well as the arrangement of items available per shelf. All he asked her to do was put her list in sequential order by shelf so that he could find each item without having to wander up and down the aisles.

His system made absolute sense to him, but was totally misunderstood by her. She thought he had deliberately dreamed up a scheme to get out of going to the grocery store! She never used his diagram and never mentioned his doing the grocery shopping again.

He assumed that this was another instance of his wife's saying that she wanted something she really didn't mean. Actually, he had been terribly disappointed that she hadn't seen the brilliance of his plan and that she hadn't appreciated his willingness to go shopping. He had "wasted" time and energy to solve her problem, and she selfishly had changed her mind!

The man and woman experienced resentment over this situation—not great enough to be a major problem, but definitely enough to scar the relationship. Later during the workshop, the couple had an opportunity to laugh about this issue that they had buried in their "never to be resolved" bin. They were relieved to know that the grocery matter was a case of misunderstanding and miscommunication rather than a deliberate lack of consideration.

TIMEWARP

To a man, time is a linear sequence of moments. It has a beginning, a middle, and an end, and it can and should be controlled.

To a woman, time is a process of discovery. It is relative and flexible; it is not always serious; and it is something that can be played with.

If a man asks a woman to be ready at seven o'clock, the woman may not consider time to be a significant issue and will be ready at *around* seven, (unless she has been trained by a man). To the man, the appointed time is serious, and if the woman is not ready at seven, it looks to him as if she is deliberately "managing" him and annoying him. The woman knows that if her appointment for seven were with another woman, she could and probably would be "late," because the other woman would not make a big deal out of it.

There is a time and place for control of time. Men can learn a great deal from women about "bending" time and relaxing more. Since time is a flexible and negotiable experience to women, it is inappropriate to expect them to change to fit the male mode or reality.

Women approach tasks from the perspective of process and discovery. Therefore, for a woman to predict the outcome of a given task in terms of time and energy is sometimes impossible, even though she may have performed the task a thousand times.

THE SHOPPING SYNDROME

Most women perceive shopping as an experience of discovery. Most men approach shopping as a task, not an adventure. When men shop, they usually have one or two items to purchase, and that is all they will look for. To look for items for which they have not allocated time, energy, and money can be a frustrating and anger-producing event.

Here again, men also expend more energy than women, because of their constant need to reorient themselves as they move from department to department, store to store or mall to mall. Women, on the other hand, are enlivened and re-energized by new sights, sounds, and aromas.

What mystifies men is that women enjoy shopping for the flow and process of it, and that they can actually spend the day shopping, not buy anything, and nevertheless return satisfied. Can you imagine a man going out to buy something—tires, for example—not finding what he set out for, and returning happy and satisfied? ("I saw these great Goodyears and some very nice Pirellis, but they just didn't have my size! Boy, was it fun!")

WANT VERSUS CAN HAVE

To a man, what he *wants* is determined by what he *can have*. In other words, a man first needs to ask a number of questions about an event before he knows if he wants to participate. Wanting to do something (desiring) and being able to do something (having the resources) are very different matters for men and women. For men, "want" and "can have" are tied together. Women perceive them as separate conditions.

She says, "Do you want to go to a party?"

He says, "When is it? Where is it? What time does it start? Who's going to be there? What will there be to eat? Do we have to bring a present?"

She says, "Never mind!" or "Can't you just answer my question? All I'm asking is if you want to go to the party!"

The woman doesn't realize that the man *is* trying to answer the question. He is asking questions in order to first determine if he is *able* to go. If he is *able* to go, he will then determine if he *wants* to go. With a man in the reverse situation, the conversation might be:

He says, "Do you want to go to a party?"

She says, "Yes."

He says, "Good. The party is Saturday night."

She says, "Oh, I can't go Saturday."

He says, "Then why did you say you wanted to go!"

Women do not confuse "want" with "can." The woman in the example gave a direct response to what she wanted to do. It was not necessary for her to see if it was possible, rational, or practical. The man didn't ask, "Are you *able* to go to the party?" He asked if she wanted to, and she answered the question he asked!

Understanding the difference between "want" and "can" further explains why husbands and boyfriends are reluctant to go "window shopping." When a man sees something he wants, he translates his desire to mean, "I think I (or you) can get it." When a woman sees something she likes, she may or may not actually want to own it. The man assumes that the woman is serious if she says she wants something, and he also assumes that she expects him to get it for her. Most men feel overwhelmed at the number of things women indicate they would buy, and they usually feel inadequate for not being able to provide her with all her "wants." I advise women to be more careful about what they say they like around a man, because six months later, the man may think he is doing her a big favor and buy it for her birthday. Although this is a sign from the man that he listened and is considerate of her wishes, she may not even remember having said she liked it.

Another example of "want" versus "can" occurred in a private consulting session with a couple who were on their way to a divorce. The decision had already been made and some people close to them had advised, "As long as you're getting divorced, why not see if you can do it in a friendly way. Go see Joe Tanenbaum."

When they did, I asked the man, "When did you know the marriage was over? When did you get really hurt? What happened?" and he began to cry.

It seems he and his wife were driving around one day, thinking about buying a house. They found a house that she said was her dream house, but they didn't have enough money to buy it. So he took a second job and worked for years getting the money for the down payment. Finally, they were able to buy the house. The day they moved in, as he turned into their new driveway, she looked down the street, saw another house, and said, "Oh, look at *that* one!" Without saying anything, he knew that she was now dissatisfied with the new house and that he would have to start saving money for the bigger house. He was devastated.

His wife was amazed by his statement. She had had no idea the impact her remark had made on her husband or on her marriage. But he couldn't recover, and that was the end of the story.

There are things women say innocently (see Chapter 11) that mean very little to them and would mean very little to other women. But to a man, the innocent comment might mean that no matter what he does, the woman will not be happy. This particular man had immediately begun to worry if his wife was going to complain every day, if she was not ever going to be satisfied, and if he had to get a second job again in order to buy her the bigger house. Women spontaneously say things that men "stuff," store, and keep track of while the woman has long forgotten what she had expressed because it had little weight to her at the time she expressed it. This demonstrates another kind of situation in which men believe that women are inconsiderate about men's energy, are always demanding, and are always asking too much without ever being satisfied.

Men genuinely want to please women and to give them what they ask for. To men, however, it seems that women often ask for things without apparent thought of what it takes to get it.

DETERMINE VERSUS DISCOVER

We've noted that men like consistency. Routines don't waste a lot of energy trying to figure out what works and what doesn't work each time. Once men figure something out, that's it for life. Isn't consistency joy? Rules have their own form of freedom.

Men need to know where, when, how, and why. One of the interesting things that comes out of the differences between "want" and "can have" are the differences between determination and discovery. Most men don't have the flexibility to discover. Discovery requires a great commitment of resources, and as one consequence of this, it's easier for men to *determine* (control) something than it is to *discover* (process) it.

For women, discovery can be an enjoyable and exciting process of change. If women don't like something, even though it may be "working," they'll change it and change it until it's better than it was—or at least different. But men will put up with something they don't like rather than expend the energy to risk a change that may not work. After all, why would anyone fix something that's not broken? What a waste of time and energy!

WHO'S IN CHARGE HERE?

For men to be comfortable, someone always needs to be in control. The controlling authority could be another man, woman, child, animal, rule, procedure, authority figure, or tradition. *Who* is in control is not as important as that *someone* or *something* is in control. Without some visible control, a man loses his center, his feeling of being grounded.

The structure of armies and most corporations (traditional male environments) is set to define lines of control so that men can relax and function well. Men are not trying to control women as much as they are just trying to avoid chaos and confusion. Men use force for control; women use intention.

Men set up armies and corporate structures so that control is not an issue, but a given. They establish control, authority, and lines of communication to preserve their energy. By having established rules and agreeing beforehand to abide by them, they also avoid being demeaned or losing face. If I'm the sergeant and he's the private, we know precisely how to deal with each other. Then women come along and say, "There are no rules" or "Let's change the rules," and expect to be appreciated and applauded!

CONTROL VERSUS INTENTION

Control

When I'm working with male groups, all the men kick back, relax, and have a good time because they know I'm in control. It is my job. If the men saw me lose control, there would be a little jostling among them and then someone would rise to the "surface" of the group and take over. At that point all the other men could relax again. As long as I'm in control, however, I'm expending energy many times faster than they. They are paying me to use my energy rather than expend theirs. As long as I can do that, they live longer because they don't have to participate.

So, remembering the example about getting to the restaurant...if the woman says to the man, "Oh, I know how to get to the restaurant," what he thinks he's hearing from her is, "I'll be in charge, and I'll make the decisions."

Another example of control might sound like this:

She says, "Okay, I know you're tired. I'll take care of everything. What would you like for dinner?"

He says, "I don't care. Whatever you make is fine with me." (He has now turned control over to her.)

She says, "Would you like the chicken or the veal?"

He says, "I don't care. You make the decision."

She says, "Potatoes or rice?"

He says, "I'll eat dead rat. Just leave me alone."

The woman doesn't hear that he has given her control because she wants relationship, communication, and partnership. I suggest that the accusation that a man always needs to be in control is not true. He needs *someone* to be in control; otherwise his energy is inappropriately expended.

If a woman says she's in control, but doesn't know the "laws" of control (according to a man), he can't trust her. Or if a man tries to give control to a woman and she won't accept it, he is automatically forced (in his reality) to get back in control. Women tend to interpret this as "big man" stuff, and if she expresses a feeling of being dominated, he thinks, "Well, you misunderstood that. What else do you misunderstand? You don't know how I'm really feeling here, so why should I trust you? You're not willing to hear what I'm saying." The same situation exists when a woman hears a man say, "Yes, I understand," even though she knows he hasn't properly heard her. The man feels the same way. Men and women are equally prone to stubbornness and righteousness. Again, there are no enemies here, just more innocent mistakes!

Intention

I describe intention as "defined direction; or an undefined technique for achieving a direction." An example of intention comes from a woman who attended one of my workshops in the Midwest. This conversation occurred during a "women-only" session when we were talking about control. This woman was perhaps five feet tall and couldn't have weighed more than 105 pounds. She said she would not talk about this topic if there had been any men besides me in the room because she knew her story had made most men and even some women feel uncomfortable.

It seems that she had always had a desire to be a captain of a rubber raft on a white-water river. She had applied at one of the boat companies and noticed that there were only big, strong men running the rafts. The management and some of the burly male employees told her politely that she was too little to control and "muscle" the boat down the river. She persisted and convinced them to accept her on a trial basis. After two years she was still a captain, and in fact, she had the best record for the least number of accidents and spills of anyone, including her powerfully built male colleagues. When I asked her how she had been able to achieve this, she warned me and the women in the room that what she was about to tell us was the truth, but that when she had tried to explain it to the men, they did not believe her.

The rivermen had assumed that her outstanding record was because she was better at some "technique" or was able to get the passengers to behave better because she was a woman. Neither was true, but she had learned to stop arguing with them. She told us that she had only two techniques. If she felt the raft going out of control or if it was getting dangerously near the rocks, she would talk to the raft and the rocks and tell them to be careful of each other. She said this technique worked most of the time. Her second technique (if the first one failed) was to tell the river to slow down, that it was going too fast.

I know that some people are very skeptical of the woman's explanation (especially men). But what if you assumed that she was telling the truth? Can you imagine what life might be like if you possessed gifts that seemed strange and unreasonable to others? I suggest that after a while, not only would you stop talking about your gifts, but you would actually begin to doubt yourself and eventually forget that you ever had that ability.

The female captain obviously could not use "force" on the river, but she could use intention. Since intention does not fit easily into the physical or intellectual modes, men have difficulty with the concept.

Intention is not consistent, reliable, or measurable; and therefore it falls prey to "rational" discussion.

Men, however, do appreciate bottom-line results. This female boat captain's remarks to the men could have been something like:

"Whether or not you believe or understand how I produce my results, I do have the statistics. I would think that you might be a little curious to learn how to improve your boating ability."

or:

"Nature gave you muscles to steer the boat and gave me intention. I think we both do pretty well for ourselves."

Another woman shared a very pertinent experience with us in one of the workshops. She told us that when she had worked for the government, she was taught a concept called Management By Objectives (MBO). She was told every year what she was supposed to do and informed of all the steps she was expected to go through to accomplish those objectives. She always produced the expected results, but she said that she really didn't go through all the required steps to accomplish the goal. (She admitted always having felt guilty about that.)

When this woman left the government job and went to work for a female executive in a small company of fifteen women, she became very confused. The women would have staff meetings every two weeks, and at her first meeting everyone sat around the conference table and talked about almost anything. There was no order to the agenda, and often more than one person talked at the same time. All the "rules of order" she had learned in her government job about conducting meetings and producing results were simply non-existent in this new setting, and it appeared to her that positive results or accomplishments would be impossible. As she watched this process in which the women seemed to be fighting each other or sometimes seemed to just gossip, she realized that it had its own momentum and value. To her surprise, by the end of the meeting the women had accomplished more work and produced more results than she had thought possible. She later realized that if a man had attended this meeting, he would have perceived this very productive process as a complete lack of process, and it would have driven him crazy!

ROMANCING THE OPPOSITE SEX

There are times when men say, "I don't know what happened to the romance in my relationship. I don't know why the sex has dropped off." My suggestion to them is very simple. I advise them to go back to "dating," to doing all the things they used to do in the early stages of their relationship: buying flowers, making loving phone calls, creating special moments in special places.

Men often get married in order to stop dating. Dating is expensive—financially, emotionally, and physically. Men can't allocate energy at that level for very long, so one of the reasons they marry is to cut the energy drain.

The woman's attitude, however, is "Oh, we're married, now it's time to play!" But men are done playing. That decision has been made. He says, "Good, we're married now. We got that handled. Forget the dating and all that stuff. Now I can get back to my job." He's ready to return to "normal" and the known elements of his life.

One piece of data that I have collected over the years is that a man marries a woman because he has decided she is THE ONE. He loves her the way she is, and she doesn't need to change. After a few months or years, the man watches the woman begin to change her life, her style, and the like, and he becomes confused. He married her for who she was, not who she was going to be. He sees the change in her as a break in their agreement of who she was when he agreed to love her. In fact, he may not love the new her, and may even feel trapped. A woman, on the other hand, marries a man for his POTENTIAL. She expects him to grow and change, and feels frustrated when he doesn't. He may feel as if she lied about her love when she married him. This is the way he was. Why doesn't she still love him that way?

One of the more interesting topics in the "women-only" part of the workshop is the discussion of sex. (Men discuss the subject of sex in their section of the workshop too, but without the detail, the humor, and the delight that women express when they are given the opportunity to have an open conversation without men in the room.)

One of the many subjects women talk about is the often-boring sexual routines of men.

As with most everything, men look for techniques that will produce results, and/or rules that will always work. For men, sex is another task. (The word "task" does not have the same connotation for men and women. Remember that men define everything in order to determine and understand the requirements.) Sex is usually one of the more pleasant tasks a man performs, but it still has a beginning, middle, and end. The "beginning" happens when one or both parties are interested in making love; the "middle" consists of his techniques; the "end" is the climax (usually his).

Once the man has established interest, he will attempt a technique that has worked in the past. The difference between a good, male lover and a man who is only interested in his own sexual satisfaction is usually just in the number of these techniques.

Once a man finds some "secret" places on the woman's body, he will go after those places with vigor. I suggest that 99% of all men would be very happy to have *one place* on his body receive all the woman's attention, and she doesn't have to get fancy! Not only does a woman have more erogenous zones than a man, but they may change from night to night, or even from moment to moment. This is very confusing to men. (If it worked yesterday, it should work today, right?) If "the place" is not working this time, the man thinks there is something on the woman's mind, or he might think she lied the previous time, when she said she liked what he was doing.

The last thing a woman wants during a romantic and spontaneous mood is to have to be rational in order to direct a man to her sensitive places. And yet, the woman may want to talk throughout the love-making. I tell women, "Don't expect that. That's real tough for a man to do." Most men who have learned to do that are actually "cycle-stealing." In other words, one second they're thinking about sex, and the next second they're thinking about what to say. But he has to keep going back to thinking of sex or he will lose his interest. My advice to men if women want talking during love-making is to say, "Wait a second, I'm doing my job here." Depending on the condition of the relationship, this could produce a good fight or a good laugh.

The man knows he is "done" when he climaxes. Not only are most women capable of multiple climaxes, but women can also be content with simply the romance, the holding, and the intimate giving and receiving of pleasure. A woman doesn't necessarily need to climax every time she makes love in order to experience satisfaction with the love-making. This concept is difficult for a man to understand, since he wouldn't be satisfied if he didn't climax. (If men were capable of multiple orgasms, they would probably never get out of bed to go to work.)

Sex to a man, like everything else, has rules and parameters. To a woman it is exploration, discovery, and adventure. Here we are again with different perceptions of reality!

CHAPTER SUMMARY

Women approach problems with an overview, using both hemispheres of the brain simultaneously.

Men need and want to segregate problems into component parts in order to arrive at solutions.

Women "see" holistically and men "see" on a highly linear basis.

Men use logic to determine trust, because for them facts build trust.

Men operate sequentially—a, b, c, d—because sequential patterns allow them to trust the "proof."

Women operate asequentially—c, a, d, b,—and can bypass unnecessary steps to solutions.

It is important for women to document their work and their ideas.

"Male" systems that can be repeated over and over again with the least number of failures and the least amount of energy expenditure make life run smoothly for men.

To men, time is a linear sequence of moments with a beginning, middle, and end; time can and should be controlled.

To women, time is a process of discovery that is both relative and flexible; it is not serious; and it is something that can be played with.

Most women approach tasks from the perspective of process and discovery.

For men, "want" and "can have" are interrelated; women perceive them as separate conditions.

Men want to please women; most men feel overwhelmed at the number of things women indicate they would buy, and it seems that women ask for things without apparent thought of what it takes to get it.

It's easier for men to *determine* something than it is to *discover* something.

For women, discovery can be an exciting process of change.

Men will put up with something they don't like rather than expend the energy to risk a change that may not work.

For men to be comfortable, someone or something always needs to be in control.

Men use force for control; women use intention.

Men establish control, authority, and lines of communication to preserve their energy.

If a man tries to give control to a woman and she won't accept it, he is automatically forced (in his reality) to take control.

Intention is not consistent, reliable, or measurable and therefore falls prey to "rational" disbelief.

Many men marry in order to alleviate the energy drain of dating.

Men look for techniques that will produce results, and/or rules that will always work.

Women have more erogenous zones than men, and they may change from day to day or even from moment to moment.

A woman doesn't necessarily need to climax every time she makes love in order to experience contentment with the love-making.

Sex to a man, like everything else, has rules and parameters.

Sex to a woman is exploration, discovery, and adventure.

11

COMMUNICATION

One of the major introductions of consciousness in a developing embryo is the formation of the corpus callosum, the bundle of nerve fibers connecting the left and right hemispheres of the brain. As we observed earlier, the female corpus callosum has more nerve fibers than that of the male, and some experiments show that women may actually have up to 40% more connectors to both sides of the brain than men. It appears that men do not receive all the information that women do. A woman's eyesight, hearing, sense of taste and smell are all more heightened than his. All of her sensitivities are more developed than his, and the information she receives is also more diffusely stored in her brain. A woman's brain is less centralized and less localized than a man's. When retrieving information, women have up to 40% greater accessing capability to both hemispheres.

The connections in a man's brain to his communication and speech center aren't as well developed as a woman's. A man goes to work for eight hours, comes home, and his wife might ask, "How was your day, Honey?" He says, "Fine." That's it—just "fine." It sounds to the woman as if he is deliberately not communicating. But to another man, that "fine" may say volumes. Another man would look at how he said "fine": how long it took him to say it, and what he looked like when he said it. All these objective signals determine what a man means. After the man says, "Fine," a woman might say, "Okay, you started, so now go on," but there's nothing for the man to go on *to!*

On the other hand, a woman can go to work for an hour, come home, and if the man says, "How was your day?" she could still be talking eight hours later. She received almost half again as much input from her five senses as the man, stored more information, and can retrieve it more quickly and with more accuracy than he, which automatically gives her more to talk about! The consensus seems to be that women talk more than men and men talk less than women. Both statements are accurate, but now we can release our judgments about the fact and become more understanding as to why this is so. The fact is, women communicate more often and more easily than men. The judgment is, women talk too much or men don't talk enough.

HOT TOPICS

Mark Sherman, associate professor of psychology, and Adelaide Haas, associate professor of communications at the State University of New York in New Paltz, have produced a very interesting study on the different responses males and females gave to 22 topics of conversation. Men (110) and women (166), ranging in age from seventeen to eighty, were given a questionnaire on their conversations they had with friends of the same sex. The topics of work, movies, and television turned out to be the most frequent areas of conversation for men and women.

The women showed more time spent than men on topics of relationship issues, families, health and reproduction, weight, eating, and clothing. The men, on the other hand, spent more time on the subjects of music, current events, and sports. The women's conversations dealt with more personal and emotional issues. Only 27% of the men said that their same-sex conversations were about emotions.

Except for sports heroes and public figures, women talked more about other women than men talked about other men.

The study did demonstrate that there are sex-based differences in what men and women think are areas of importance. When a topic was of no interest to one sex it was usually described as boring or a waste of time.

The study also found that it was not the topic of conversation as much as the way the conversation was delivered and the purpose of the conversation that caused differences. The men felt that the purpose of their conversations with other men was for the freedom they felt, the ability to play, and the comradery they felt. Not having to be so careful about what they said was the most frequent response men gave as to what they enjoyed most about their conversations with other men. In addition, the men thought that the conversations were more fast-paced, contained more humor, and seemed to be more practical. The men used their time in a very informal setting with other men to learn about their cars, or how to handle money matters.

When women were asked what they liked best about talking with other women, many mentioned ease and comradery, as did the men. However, the definitions of these terms were significantly different. To women, ease and comradery meant empathy and understanding (which involves *careful listening*, as well as the ability to communicate). Women wanted to know that they were not alone, and they liked the feeling of sharing with and understanding each other without devoting attention to worrying about sexual connotations or undertones.

The women indicated that sensitivity to emotions was an important part of their same-sex conversations, but the men attached little or no importance to emotions as part of theirs. Women spoke of their female conversations, not as something they merely liked, but something they truly needed. While 63% of the women called their same-sex conversations important or necessary, only 43% of the men said their own same-sex conversations were important or necessary.

Women were also more likely to call a friend on the telephone just to talk. Only 14% of the women said they never called just to talk, while over 40% of the men said they never called a friend just to chat.

In general, the men expected women to interact with them in the same "stay-on-the-surface" (non-emotional), fast-paced style as their male friends would. Their conversations were meant to give or receive practical information and be fun. The women expected the men to be interested in more personal and emotional issues without the "bottom-line" men always seem to need. Women also expected their conversations to be fun, but obviously the definitions of fun are different.

CROSS TALK

All of the data from my workshops confirms that a woman expects conversations to be practical and fun, but she also expects them to be a major source of emotional support as she attempts to understand herself and others. When a woman starts an intimate relationship with a man, she then assumes that she can be open (and therefore vulnerable). She assumes that she does not have to guard against being misunderstood, so she begins to share her intimate feelings with her new male partner as if she were talking to her best woman friend. What usually happens, however, is that his responses are all wrong for her. Instead of making her feel better, he makes her feel worse. He tends to be direct and practical, but what she is seeking more than anything else is an empathic listener. Since she expects him to listen as another woman would listen (or in the way she would listen to him if he were talking), she is likely to be surprised and angered by his "immediate solution" approach. She takes his "fix-it" attitude as a personal rejection, or she suspects he is making a statement about her intelligence or relative importance to him. From his reality, he is talking to her as he would expect her (or his best friend) to talk to him.

Obviously, this same misunderstanding happens in the work place, where women assume that after relationships and friendships are established, they can be vulnerable with men. After a few difficult experiences, they quickly learn to protect themselves from the men and the male-trained women.

GETTING ATTENTION

Most teachers claim that girls participate and are called on in class as often as boys, but a three-year study, "Sexism in the Schoolroom of the 80's," found that this is not true. Vocally, boys clearly dominate the classroom. In the study, teachers and administrators were shown a film of a classroom discussion and were then asked who was talking more. The teachers overwhelmingly said the girls were. In reality, however, the boys in the film were out-talking the girls at a ratio of *three to one*. Even the female educators were unable to spot these sex differences until they counted and coded who was talking and who was just watching. Whether the subject was language arts and English or math and science, boys consistently received more than their share of teacher attention.

The research also showed that boys were more assertive in the classroom and were *eight times* more likely than girls to call out answers. While girls sat patiently with their hands raised, boys literally grabbed teacher attention. (Does this sound like your staff meetings? Social gatherings? Family meetings?)

Although girls are ahead of boys in reading and basic computation when they start school, boys score higher than girls in both areas by the time they graduate.

When asked to explain the reason for having obtained poor scores, girls were more likely to attribute failure to internal factors such as ability, or not being prepared, or not having understood the questions— all inclusive deductions. The boys, on the other hand, attributed their failures to external factors, such as bad luck, distractions around them, or the test not having been administered properly—all exclusive justifications.

FANNING THE FLAME OF BLAME

When a man wants to interact with a problem, the first thing he does is look outside himself to identify the cause of the problem, because men use objective reality to determine cause and effect. When the man looks outside himself, however, the woman usually feels accused and blamed, because women always look inside first: "What am I doing wrong?" "Am I nagging too much?" "How can I improve?"

From a man's perspective, if he says, "It's your fault. You fix it," she may go ahead and fix it! He's no longer involved, and she has just saved him the bother of dealing with it.

Since the woman is quicker and usually more willing to look inside first, the man assumes she has taken responsibility for the situation and that he doesn't need to look further into the problem. The woman, however, erroneously assumes that her partner is also looking within to see how he is contributing to the problem. If the woman can't fix the problem alone, she will look outside for help and see what she needs to do. If the woman "objectively" responds to the man's accusations (and the solution not found in her), then and only then will the man look inside. These misassumptions generally translate into: 1) he is inconsiderate and unwilling to admit fault; 2) she has low self-esteem since she so easily finds fault with herself.

DYNAMICS OF DEFINITIONS

The words and language used by men and women are very different. It is easier for men to understand men, and easier for women to understand each other. We miss much of the substance of mixed-gender conversations because we automatically define words differently.

"Commitment," "responsibility," "sell," and "bargain," for example, are highly charged words that have different meanings in different cultural contexts.

Dictionaries are a left-brain (typically male) invention for dealing with complex notions and abstractions. The dictionary is useful to men in settling rational arguments because definitions eliminate the need for them to rely on intuition or a "sense" of what is being said.

If no word exists in your vocabulary for a corresponding personal experience of a feeling, attitude, or physical experience, you would obviously have difficulty relating to that word. For example, if you had never heard of or experienced snow, or any other form of frozen water, it would be a frustrating experience for both of us if I tried to describe snow to you. I might even feel justified in labeling you naive, ignorant, or stupid.

Many public speakers are aware of this communication difference when addressing all-female, all-male, and mixed-gender audiences. Although the information is the same, an entirely different talk is required to "reach" the different genders. When I am speaking from a male viewpoint, men understand me, but many (if not all) of the women are confused. If I speak from the female viewpoint, the women immediately understand me, but the men become confused, bored, or frustrated. In a mixed-gender audience, half the participants are likely to feel frustrated and dissatisfied. Group dynamics are drastically different (and usually more comfortable) if the groups are segregated by sex. However, with re-education and training, these differences can be overcome.

In my seminars where both men and women are present, it is common for all the men to be confused about some experience I am describing to the women. While the women can relate to the topic, the men are waiting (and sometimes struggling) to understand what the women are relating to. Men have actually accused the women in the room of a conspiracy to confuse them. Every time a woman would attempt to explain to the men what we were talking about, the men just became more frustrated. This demonstrates our inability to relate to experiences that we personally cannot even imagine. The same confusion happens with women when I am describing a male experience. The women assume that the men and I are deliberately *not* describing the experience in a way that they can relate to.

WOMEN AS COMMUNICATORS

Researchers Doreen Kimura and Jeannette McGlone at Western Ontario's University Hospital have been working on the different effects of brain damage (from tumors and strokes) in right-handed men and women. Their findings show that women are much less susceptible to brain injuries than men because the male brain is so laterally specialized. Damage to one or the other of a man's hemispheres virtually always produces a loss of language (left) or spatial skills (right). Since the woman's brain is not organized in the same way, her loss of spatial and language skills as a result of brain injury is not as common. The study also indicated quite a different distribution of language mapping in the brains of men and women.

Using radioactive gas, Ruben Gur, an Israeli scientist, has shown that male and female brains are differently constituted and differently supplied with blood when at work on certain tasks.

Women are better at almost all the skills that involve words (fluency, verbal reasoning, written prose and reading). A woman's memory of words and language is also better. Males outnumber females by three to one in remedial reading classes.

The slightest brain damage occurring during or after birth has a far more debilitating effect on boys than it does on girls. Brain damage almost always occurs in the hemisphere in which boys are less well organized, the left. It is generally not the visual-spatial abilities (located in the right hemisphere) that are affected, but the left hemisphere, so language control and language skills suffer. Boys are four to five times more likely to suffer from language disorders and disabilities than girls.

Boys are more likely (five to one) to stutter when the left hemisphere loses control during speech. Boys are also more likely to be autistic (four to one), often with complete absence of left-hemisphere language. And boys are more likely to suffer from two developmental disorders: aphasia (extreme difficulty learning to talk by a five-to-one ratio) and dyslexia (extreme difficulty with reading and writing by a six-to-one ratio).

HOW MEN DEAL WITH COMMUNICATION

I have defined three stages that men go through on their way to communication. First, they mull, then store, and then communicate.

Mull

A man puts the problem or situation on a "back burner." If the problem can be resolved with little attention or energy, he is ahead of the game. He will wait to see if the problem goes away or gets resolved with the least amount of energy that can be expended. (Mulling is different than thinking.) Men are not moved to action unless it appears that there is no alternative. Mulling can take a few moments or many years. While in the mulling stage, the man does not feel it is useful or necessary to communicate yet. If the problem resolves on its own, it would have been a "waste" of time and energy (from a male point of view) to bother to communicate. If the problem does not resolve by the mulling process, the man goes on to the next stage.

Store/Stuff

Issues that cannot be resolved by mulling are actually stored or "stuffed" in a man's body. The results of this second stage are not surprising: Men suffer from stress-related illnesses such as heart disease, ulcers, and other physical problems far more so than do women. Men die on an average of eight years sooner than women from the fifteen major disease-related deaths. In spite of the statistical data demonstrating that it would be to men's benefit to communicate, it still appears to them that the easiest solution is to keep problems inside. Most men ignore the many early warning signs that would let them know when their bodies need attention. Male bodies evolved by ignoring pain, but this necessary feature for fighting battles is a potentially harmful carry-over into most men's lifestyles today. From a male perspective, one still has some control of the situation as long as the problem is within one's grasp (even if it means that one's body becomes ill); it is *his* problem and he doesn't have to bother anyone else with it. Knowing how much trouble it is for him to resolve problems, he does not want to burden anyone else unless he is going out of control. If he sees this condition occurring and has no other alternative, he may then elect to go to the final stage.

Explode/Communicate

When all else has failed, a man will resort to communicating. This final stage takes the most amount of energy, and communication may not be necessary if mulling and stuffing work. This "last resort" is not a comfortable stage for a man. His communication skills are not as developed as a woman's, and his admission that he has a problem which he can't solve is associated with the discomfort of being "out of control."

For example, a man could be standing in the kitchen with his back to the door when he hears his wife (who may have just walked into the kitchen) slamming a cabinet door. By the time he turns around, she is out of the kitchen. Because the door slammed, he is certain (a mistaken assumption) that there is a problem. He knows she is angry (it doesn't even occur to him to question it), and he now has one of three options:

1. Ignore it;
2. Go and help her out of her "mood" with support; or
3. Go and fix her.

If he ignores her, he is sure her anger will just fester until he will have to deal with it sooner or later, so he might as well go on to option two or three.

If he decides to "help" her, the following conversation may occur:

He says, "Honey, what's wrong?"

She says, "Nothing. Why?"

(The man is now sure that her denial is proof that there is something wrong, so he asks again.)

He says, "No, really. What's the matter?"

The woman begins to lose her patience, begins to wonder what's wrong with the man, and unknowingly furthers the ensuing fight by saying:

"Well, what's wrong with *you?*"

Given her response, the man is now positive that she has a problem, and the fight (or silence) begins.

Remember, this altercation started because the man "knew" two facts (neither of which may have been true):

1. She deliberately slammed the cabinet door. (Men don't accidently slam doors.)
2. Slamming the door meant she was angry (and given his orientation that the world revolves around him—his "spot"—her anger had something to do with him).

When I present this situation in my workshops and ask the men, "Why do you think she slammed the door?" Without prompting, 100% of the men respond, "She's angry!". When I ask the women's interpretation of the same situation, they give me almost as many explanations as there are women in the room. The women don't make the same beginning assumption as the men. Here are some of their responses:

"She may not have realized that the door was slammed."

"She might have been upset with something else and the slamming of the door released her anger. The upset was over before she left the kitchen."

"She was having fun with the door."

"Maybe she was upset with him, but so what? Why did he have to make a big deal out of it?"

If the man tries his third familiar option, which is to fix her, he begins with the same conversation but accelerates it.

He says, "Honey, what's wrong?"

She says, "Nothing. Why?"

The man is now sure that her denial is proof that there is something wrong. So he asks again:

"No, really. What's the matter."

She says, "There's nothing wrong!"

He says, "Then why did you slam the cabinet door?"

She says, "I didn't slam the cabinet door!"

He says, "I was in the kitchen. I heard you slam the door. Don't tell me I didn't hear the door slam! So why did you slam it?"

She says, "Okay, okay! Let's say I did slam the door. What's the big deal?"

He says, "Don't try to pacify me. I know you slammed the door. Why can't you just admit it?"

Seeing no way out of this conversation, the woman now either walks away (which just avoids this "fight" for the moment or accelerates it), or she says (in a convincing tone):

"Okay, you're right. I slammed the door. What's the problem?"

He says, "So what are you upset about?"

She says, "Who said I was upset?"

He says, "You just admitted that you slammed the door! We've already established that, so what are you angry about?"

This argument could go around and around and around to even greater misunderstanding. It doesn't occur to the man that his assumption may have been inaccurate (in order to slam the door, the woman must be angry). It doesn't occur to the woman that the man has no alternative but to assume that she is angry. (*He* certainly would be, if he slammed the door.)

HOW WOMEN DEAL WITH COMMUNICATION

One of the basic problems in communication is that men believe women have already gone through the same process they go through in order to communicate. That is, a man will be sure the woman has already tried to "mull" it and was unsuccessful, has tried to "stuff" it and couldn't, and so consequently she must be in trouble and out of control. Women's communications are perceived as requests for solutions, since, according to male reality, one doesn't communicate unless one needs help!

Expressing to Express/Expressing to Resolve

Have you ever listened to a man discussing an issue with another man by phone? It might sound like, "Fire the guy!" or "Sell your car!" A woman's reaction to hearing this might be, "That's it? That's a friendship? Your friend had a problem and *that's* all you did?" Well, from the man's point of view, his friend was obviously out of control, or he wouldn't have called. He doesn't know what to do, and a true friend will objectively tell him what to do to get back on track. He didn't want to "talk." He just wanted to be told what to do so he could get back in control, because being out of control is very expensive. A man's inability to resolve an emotional or intellectual issue takes a lot of his energy and focus.

Men have asked women for this same treatment, but then the women "talk" instead of "answering." Men want the bottom line: "What should I do?" (He'll either do it or not, but just give him your answer!)

Men become confused when women communicate about an issue, because sometimes women want it resolved, and sometimes they don't! Sometimes a woman doesn't know whether she wants it resolved until after she's talked about it. Unfortunately, she can't always tell the man in advance if she wants the issue resolved or not.

In other words, sometimes women express just to express. They're just communicating. It's a way they have of interacting with the world. And they're just talking; they're not even expecting an answer because they don't know they need an answer. They're looking for self-expression.

While women sometimes express to express, men almost always express to resolve. When a woman communicates a problem to a man without providing a solution or directions to a solution, the man will immediately begin to try to resolve the "issue." In the "express-to-express" mode, the woman might be talking simply to keep in touch with the man and doesn't realize that the man is trying to help with a "problem." She may not perceive any problem at all, in fact, and she may aggravate the situation or "insult" the man by saying, "Who asked you to help?"

Meeting formats have been designed and defined by men for their own comfort. There are planning meetings, creative meetings, information meetings, etc. Men need to compartmentalize their thinking in order to know what rules to use. And there are generally plenty of those, both spoken and unspoken.

Men look for consistency to see what and who they can trust. When women "express to express," men must then test to see if they're telling the truth, because according to male reality, it looks as if women lie much too often. Or at the very least, it looks as if women are not concerned whether or not something is true. It may not be an actual lie, but women don't seem to be as worried as men about accuracy.

To a great degree, what makes women a problem for men is inconsistency. But because women are inclusive, they don't need to be consistent to be happy (except in the case of male-trained women).

Let me paraphrase an interview I watched with a psychologist and a couple. The psychologist asked the woman, "What do you need? What's lacking in the relationship?"

The woman said, "I need him to say, 'I love you' more often."

The psychologist asked the man "Well, do you love her?"

And the man said, "Of course." (Remember men's objective reality: the proof of his love is that he is physically there. "Actions speak louder than words." The same situation occurs when a woman asks a man, "Do you like your meal?" He says, "I'm eating it, aren't I?")

The psychologist continued, "Well, do you tell her that you love her?"

"Of course, about three times a week." (That's what he had allocated.)

"But you love her all week, don't you?" the psychologist probed.

"Yes," the husband said.

"Well, why don't you tell her? She needs to hear it more often," the psychologist suggested.

The husband replied, "Because, it's not natural. I tell her three times. If I told her the fourth time, it would be phony. It would be forced. It wouldn't be natural. If I said 'I love you' the fourth time, it would only be to please her. I would feel like it was a lie.''

Male logic. The forcing of ''I love you'' made it a lie. The fact that it was true underneath wasn't important. It was the fact that this man didn't say it on his own that made it "forced." He felt manipulated by the woman and therefore didn't honor her request, even though pleasing her would have made his life with her a great deal easier.

Over time, men tend to become less and less communicative than they were at the beginning of the relationship because there seems to be no end to a woman's need to communicate.

SOLUTIONS TO COMMUNICATION PROBLEMS

The following principles apply to individuals or groups with differing points of view who are ready to solve their communication problems:

1. Develop an attitude of trust—that is, assume the other person is telling you the truth.

This doesn't mean that you should automatically believe what is said, but that you maintain an open-minded approach to communication. Sometimes people will say something from their point of view that doesn't make sense from your perspective. For example, you may be feeling very warm and you ask your friend how he/she feels. They say, ''I feel cold.'' If you do not think the room is cold, a normal reaction would be, ''How can you possibly be cold? It must be eighty degrees in here! What's wrong with you?'' However, if you assume your friend is telling the truth, a ''win-win'' solution can be arranged. If not, the conversation is likely to become bogged down in determining who is ''right,'' or who needs to change. The relationship at this point could very well end in disagreement, animosity, or cold silence. The alternative can be:

''How do you feel?''

''Cold.''

''That's interesting...I feel warm.'' or ''Would you like to borrow my jacket? I'm feeling warm.''

2. Assume that the other person is trying to communicate and also trying to understand your communication.

Most people are trying to get along and are anxious to have situations resolved. Like you, they are probably doing the best they can with the information they have. Among the thousands of individuals I have worked with, I have only encountered a small handful of deliberately inconsiderate human beings.

3. When there is a miscommunication or misunderstanding, treat the other person as if he or she is from another culture. Assume that the miscommunication is not an attempt to demean or manipulate you, but a genuinely different way of perceiving, based on difference alone.

Example: Someone approaches you who is just learning the English language. He or she might confuse past and future tenses, or perhaps use the wrong pronouns, or might say "inside" when they really mean "outside." (You could be called "not ugly" instead of "physically attractive.") Generally, there is no intention to confuse, insult, or demean when this happens. You then inform the person that a particular phrase (or behavior) is inappropriate, and you give them the opportunity to change. This is true also about titles. We assume that others should know how we want to be addressed. A man could be referred to as man, male, guy, sir, mister, his first or last name. A woman could be referred to as female, woman, Ms., Miss, Mrs., ma'am, her first or last name. I don't believe we have the right to be annoyed with the way we are addressed until we have informed another how we wish to be addressed and give them ample time to adjust to our needs.

CAUSES FOR INAPPROPRIATE COMMUNICATION

In our day-to-day conversational exchanges, inappropriate communication takes place for a number of reasons:

1. Deliberate attempts are made to annoy or insult you (as a form of retribution or revenge).
2. Your requests for appropriate communication (or behavior) are understood, but the other person does not know how to alter his/her behavior to make the change. (They know you are upset, but they don't see an alternative way of speaking.)
3. For whatever reason, the person cannot (is not able) to make the change.

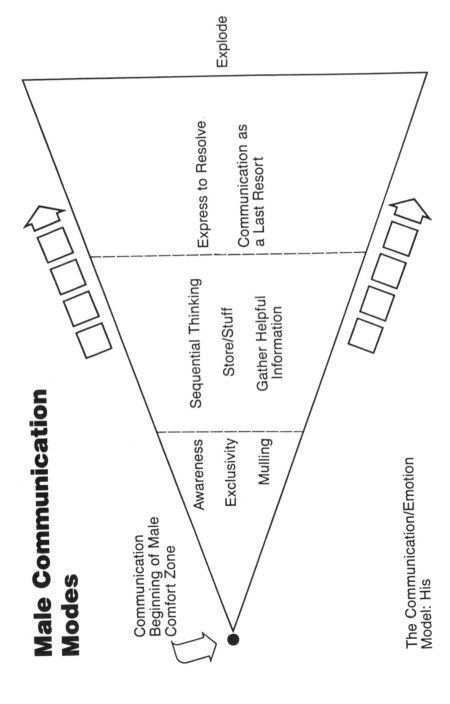

Male Communication Modes

Communication
Beginning of Male
Comfort Zone

Awareness

Exclusivity

Mulling

Sequential Thinking

Store/Stuff

Gather Helpful
Information

Express to Resolve

Communication as
a Last Resort

Explode

The Communication/Emotion
Model: His

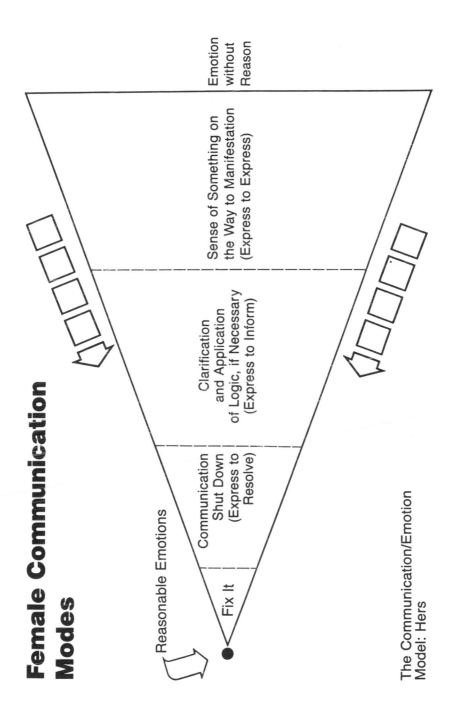

Female Communication Modes

Emotion without Reason

Sense of Something on the Way to Manifestation (Express to Express)

Clarification and Application of Logic, if Necessary (Express to Inform)

Communication Shut Down (Express to Resolve)

Reasonable Emotions

Fix It

The Communication/Emotion Model: Hers

4. The person is willing to make the change, but the change is not happening quickly enough for you.

5. You may be overly sensitive or narrow in your perceptions. (For example, you may not want to be called "thin" because it has a special negative meaning to you.)

Unfortunately, we often overlook the last reason (our own perceptions) and usually assume the first (that a person is deliberately trying to annoy us and that they are succeeding!).

If you were going to visit someone in another country (i.e. Japan), you would probably want to learn as much as possible about that culture in order to show respect for your host's traditions. If a cultural mistake is made, or a misunderstanding arises, both individuals would attempt to explain the misunderstanding and would attempt to reinterpret the action as innocent and unintentional. You would probably apologize and try to correct your speech or behavior.

In this actual foreign setting, you would intellectually know that neither cultural reality is "better" than the other. But emotionally, all of us tend to be a little self-righteous about our own reality. For example, your thought or opinion might be that people should sit on chairs at a table, not on the floor; or that people should not go barefoot except at home or that bowing to someone during an introduction is subservient. The point is that your reality may work for you, but not for everyone else.

Simple miscommunications can be greatly alleviated if individuals want to resolve the misunderstanding and are willing to listen and learn. The misunderstandings between men and women are usually as innocent as cultural misunderstandings. However, since we assume similar motivation and interpretation, we usually engage in feeling hurt, angry, or impatient while we neglect apologies and attempts at real understanding.

CHAPTER SUMMARY

Men do not receive all the sensory information that women do.

Women have up to 40% greater accessing capability to both hemispheres of the brain.

Women's conversational topics tend to be closer to the self and more emotional than men's.

There are areas of personal importance that the opposite sex is simply not interested in, and in fact, may deride.

The differences in preferred topics of conversation are not as likely to damage intimate male/female relationships as are the differences in the *style* and *function* of the conversation.

Male conversations are an informal method of sharing solutions to everyday problems.

Sensitivity to emotions is an important part of women's same-sex conversations, but men attach little or no importance to emotions as elements of theirs.

Men expect fast-paced conversations that stay on the surface, that enable them to give and receive practical tips, and that are usually pragmatic or fun.

Women expect conversations to be a major source of emotional support as they attempt to understand themselves and others.

Women are likely to be surprised and angered by men's "immediate solution" approach.

Vocally, boys dominate the classroom.

When men want to interact with a problem, the first thing they do is look outside themselves to identify the cause of the problem.

Woman first look inside themselves to identify the apparent cause of a problem.

Much of the substance of mixed-gender conversations is missed because men and women automatically define words differently.

Group dynamics are drastically different (and sometimes more comfortable) if segregated by sex.

Women are much less susceptible to brain injuries than men because the male brain is so laterally specialized.

Women are better than men at almost all the skills involving words.

Males are four to five times more likely to suffer from language disorders and disabilities than females.

Men have three modes of dealing with issues that may require communication:

- mull
- store/stuff

- explode/communicate

Women's communications are perceived by men as requests for solutions, since, according to male reality, one doesn't communicate unless one needs help.

Women sometimes express to express, but men always express to resolve.

Inconsistency makes women confusing to men.

Solutions to communication problems:
- develop an attitude of trust
- assume the other person is trying to communicate and also trying to understand your communication
- treat the other person as if he or she is from another culture

Causes for inappropriate communication:
- deliberate attempts to annoy or insult someone
- requests for appropriate communication (or behavior) are understood, but the other person does not know how to make the change
- the person cannot (or is not able to) make the change
- there is willingness to make the change, but the change is not taking place quickly enough
- you may be overly sensitive or narrow in your perceptions

Your reality may work for you, but not for everyone else.

12

EMOTION

Emotions do not come from the "rational" portion of the brain. The area of the brain associated with emotion is larger in women than it is in men. Women, therefore, have a distinct advantage over men in their ability to relate to and express emotions. Just as men have developed and counted on their physical strength over the centuries, so women have developed and depended on their emotional strength.

Most psychological research shows that women tend to be the intimacy experts. (Intimacy is defined here as revealing feelings and being able to confide freely in another person.) Many men regard intimacy in terms of what they do (action) instead of what they say (talk).

As we noted in the last chapter, for women, love means expressing love (talking about/subjective reality). For men, it often means simply being present (physical demonstration/objective reality). Remember our earlier examples:

She says, "Do you love me?"

He says, "I'm here, aren't I?"

or

She says, "Do you like your dinner?"

He says, "I'm eating it, aren't I?"

131

The woman assumes that since the man is not saying anything, then nothing is real. She is waiting for a verbal expression as reality. A man assumes that, because objective reality exists for him, talk is unnecessary.

Women take responsibility for caretaking much more than men do. In 83% of all American homes, it is women who make the medical and health-care decisions. They are responsible for the care of children, husbands, parents, and friends. They run their households, shop, cook meals, nurture everyone through flu and chicken pox, arrange family dinners, and make sure that relatives receive birthday cards on the right dates.

Women are also better than men at "stroking," a term used to describe nonphysical support, such as soothing hurt feelings, moral support, praise, and encouragement.

Women assume that men are capable of giving the same amount of emotional support that they give, and therefore, women tend to be less satisfied with love and marriage than men. In surveys, men at all ages say they are happier in love than women are. More husbands than wives say they would marry the same spouse if they could do it again, and fewer men than women believe that they will ever be divorced.

Women *appear* to have more emotional problems than men because they communicate more openly about their concerns and fears. Women are also much more sensitive to their emotional environment and are more willing to instigate changes. Seventy percent of people who seek out-patient psychotherapy are women, and women outnumber men three to one at workshops and seminars on personal growth and relationship issues.

A 1970 study showed that when women's reactions differ from men's, therapists tend to see women as "wrong" rather than "different." When the therapists were asked to identify what made a man, a woman, and an adult healthy, most of them described the healthy man and the healthy adult as having the same personality traits. The healthy woman was described as having contrasting characteristics, but according to the study, the women could be regarded only as healthy females and not as healthy female adults.

Flor-Henry, professor of clinical psychology at the University of Alberta, suggests that for women, depression and phobias obviously go together. Phobias attack the right hemisphere of the brain, which, in females, is organized more precariously than that in males. Some phobias usually appear in women only during their child-bearing years. These fears may include anything and everything that could be considered dangerous in the environment: heights, closets, spaces, water, snakes, and so on. It might be that these fears are instilled in a woman for the protection of her child or future children. And they obviously have to do with mood, movement, and visual/spatial skill—right hemisphere functions. Flor-Henry also states that the sex drive is affected.

The researchers found that women are better than men at getting emotional support or guidance from people around them. It is important for women to continue to encourage men to communicate more openly during stressful periods. Men need to experiment in learning to become comfortable about talking to people during their troubled times.

It has been suggested by Flor-Henry and others that there may be a mechanism in the brain that is activated during infancy which allows infants to cry freely and to relieve stress. Whatever its cause, that freedom is overruled later in life, particularly after puberty. Though only a correlation, it's interesting to note that levels of testosterone are low at birth (when crying occurs freely), but they rise in boys during adolescence, suggesting that hormonal changes might account for the overruling of the average teenaged boy's freedom to cry.

HORMONES AND EMOTIONS

The relationship between our behavior and our body chemistry is just beginning to be explored. Hockey players who respond aggressively to threat in their sport have higher levels of testosterone than the average population of males. Prisoners with long histories of violent crime also seem to have higher testosterone levels than the normal prison population. Young males, whose levels of testosterone are highest, commit almost all the violent crimes, many of which are sex-related. Many more men than women combine sexual deviance and aggression.

After giving birth, seven percent of new mothers suffer for weeks, even months, from severe depression and complete loss of sexual interest. (I suspect this figure will increase as women learn more about this condition and are better able to communicate about it; and as physicians and psychologists become more accurate in their diagnoses.)

British psychiatrist Katharina Dalton believes that premenstrual tension affects four out of ten women to at least some extent, and that for eight days before and during menstruation, it affects one of those four seriously. The symptoms include brooding, lethargy, depression, loss of memory and emotional control; they also have been identified as factors in increased incidents of quarrels, accidents, suicides, baby battering, and crime. Those women who use birth control pills, according to Dr. Dalton, seem to be more severely affected than others.

The symptoms are all too often regarded by the lovers, husbands, and doctors of the affected women—and even by the women themselves—as psychological in origin. Consequently, it has been the woman's responsibility to "fix" these symptoms, which have often led to the breakup of marriages and/or feelings of severely lowered self-esteem in females.

THE DOUBLE WHAMMY

Since women have two X chromosomes, they are more sensitive to moods and temperament than men, and they generally lack volatility. In rare cases, some males are born with two X chromosomes, *as well as* the Y chromosome, and are unusually aggressive (Klinefelter's Syndrome).

Females given male hormones may become masculinized, but they do not lose their feminine characteristics. In fact, there are no female traits that can be suppressed by exposing the female fetus to male hormones. Males and altered females are simply females who have had male characteristics superimposed over their female base. The female base remains and is more fully protected than the male. Nature can afford a wide variation of males, but since females are the bearers of children, nature does as much as possible to protect a potential child-bearing woman.

THE EMOTIONAL EDGE

Men begin to experience emotions on the physical plane through their perceptions of reasons and causes.

Women discover emotions after having entered the physical plane from an area I call "No Man's Land." What I mean by "No Man's Land" is that "place" in female reality where men cannot reach. I suggest that men who venture into "No Man's Land" and try to stay there become disoriented and confused, or they become incapable of relating to the physical realm. (Extremely creative men or spiritual masters usually need aides to provide for their survival.) Women, on the other hand, can operate from "No Man's Land" and still fully function in the physical plane.

One of the most common complaints I receive from women is that men tend to be either stuck to "the spot" (immovable, inflexible) or are so near the edge of the physical plane that they are unreliable, confused, overly emotional, or dysfunctional. There seems to be no happy medium, only extremes. Unfortunately, finding the "superman" of men is about as unlikely as finding the "wonderwoman" of women.

Reasonable Emotions

Men always have a way to backtrack in order to discover a reason (intellectual) for their emotions, and they expect women to be able to do the same. If a situation (good or bad) is not resolved for the man, he begins to use up greater and greater amounts of energy until he reaches a solution or reaches the "wall" of physical reality.

A man has to be willing to lose control of some physical orientation in order to reach beyond the limits of objective reality into the subjective realm. A woman, however, can travel between realities freely, as long as the demands on the physical plane do not become overwhelming or too focused.

Women assume that men would feel better if they were as emotional as women are. But for men, operating in the emotional realm depletes their energy and thereby weakens them.

Being Appropriate

Men do not deny that they cry or feel emotions. However, time and place are important to a man's expression of emotions, and *his* definition of what is appropriate needs to be respected (e.g., not in the line at the movie theater!).

Women perceive the expression of emotions as a positive sign, but men regard emotions as warning signals. Women utilize emotions as a stage that a vision goes through on its way to manifestation. (See "Communication/Emotion Model" in Chapter 11.) A man's attention, however, is on resolving what he considers to be a problem.

Emotions as Monitors

To a great extent, emotions in the male are simply a monitor of his energy reserves. If emotional energy is present, the man uses more energy than if no emotion is present. If a man stays "neutral" (without emotion), he assumes that his decisions will be more accurate and that he will live longer because he uses less energy from his reserves.

The energy drain that men experience in order to deal with emotions is not limited to the negative expression of feelings. Men allocate energy for having fun, as well as for working out problems. They plan ahead and want to know as many facts as possible, even when they are vacationing. Women are constantly amazed that men use the same techniques and "rigidity" to enjoy their vacations that they do on the job. Part of the fun for a man is to plan for and know that he has the energy reserves to enjoy himself! However, a man can only "be happy" for a limited amount of time before he needs to retreat to his "spot" to re-energize.

Planned Spontaneity

At a recent talk, I mentioned that men are never spontaneous (excluding men who are out of balance and confused), and one of the women in the room pointed to her husband and said, "My husband did something last night that was spontaneous!" I told her I didn't want to start an argument between her and her husband, because I know how much women want their men to be spontaneous. I went on to assure her that he hadn't been truly spontaneous in the same way *she* understood spontaneity. (When men say they are being spontaneous, they mean that they didn't plan or think about something for as long as usual, but they did think about it!) The husband spoke up and said, "Joe's right. I did think about it beforehand." His wife turned to him and said, "No, I know you were being spontaneous last night."

I could feel his dilemma. He could either lie and say, "Yes, I was spontaneous," in which case he would please his wife; or he could do what he did (which took a lot of courage) and disagree with his wife at the risk of upsetting her.

This example demonstrates the difficulty we have in listening to each other. The woman enjoyed what her husband did "spontaneously" (she wouldn't tell us what it was, but the smile on both their faces was great!). The fact that he had planned less than usual was fun enough for him, but if she conceded her belief that he was being spontaneous, she would have to give up some of her enjoyment of his behavior on the previous night.

Stress for Success

A major cause of stress in males is related to excessive focus on a problem that is not being resolved in the expected amount of time with the allotted amount of energy. Men will sometimes create stressful situations in order to test themselves and those around them, and/or to determine limitations.

For most men, stress occurs under the following conditions:

1. When his ability to focus has been taken to the extreme, and he becomes "exclusive" to the problem (that is, when there is no flow or exchange of energy);
2. When he hasn't removed the causes for the continued focus;
3. When he hasn't removed himself from the stress-producing environment.

Women who have entered the job market and have placed themselves in stressful situations are beginning to manifest male symptoms of stress. Under normal situations, women's estrogen levels protect them from heart attacks and stress-related diseases. However, the occurrence of "burnout" is extremely high. There is also a high divorce rate among female executives—higher than the equivalent for male executives, who usually have supportive female relationships (that is, relationships with partners who are not themselves executives).

What has been dubbed the Type A personality (usually associated with workaholics) demonstrates a chronic sense of urgency regarding time and is hard-driving, competitive, extroverted, and aggressive. Type A's are particularly at risk from the damaging effects of stress.

Studies by psychologist Marian Frankenhauser at the University of Stockholm have shown that Type A females, when solving work-related problems, simply don't show the increase in heart rate, blood pressure, and adrenaline that Type A males do. And even when their overall health picture is the same, Type A women don't suffer as many heart attacks.

Women are more likely to experience stress as a result of emotional situations in their lives as opposed to the kinds of "paper problems" that produce stress in men.

Scientists working with male laboratory animals have shown that successful sexual dominance and the successful maintenance of large territory is associated with high blood pressure and hardening of the arteries, measurable signs of the effects of stress. The researchers also found that the animals "at the top" had higher levels of testosterone.

When women experience setbacks, failures, or emotional pressures, they don't go into "overdrive" the way men do; they respond in the opposite way, by expressing (communicating as a release) or succumbing to depression (internalizing what they may have done to create the problem).

CHAPTER SUMMARY

Women have a distinct advantage over men in their ability to relate to and express emotions.

Many men view intimacy in terms of what they do (action) instead of what they say (talk).

Women take responsibility for caretaking much more often than men do.

Men are more satisfied with love and marriage than women.

Women are better than men at getting emotional support or guidance from people around them.

Young males, whose levels of testosterone are highest, commit almost all the violent crimes.

Many more men than women combine sexual deviance and aggression.

Nature does as much as possible to protect a potential child-bearing woman.

Men begin to experience emotions on the physical plane through perceiving reasons and causes.

Women discover emotions after having entered the physical plane from "No Man's Land."

Men give up control of physical orientation in order to reach beyond the limits of objective reality into the subjective realm.

Women can travel freely between realities, as long as the demands on the physical plane do not become overwhelming or too focused.

Time and place are important to a man's expression of emotions, and his definition of what is appropriate needs to be respected.

Women perceive emotions as a positive sign, while men regard emotions as warning signals.

To a great extent, emotions in the male are simply a monitor of his energy reserves.

Stress for males is related to excessive focus on a problem which is not being resolved in the expected amount of time with the allotted amount of energy.

Men will sometimes create stressful situations in order to test themselves and those around them, and/or to determine limitations.

Type A females, when solving work-related problems, don't show the increase in heart rate, blood pressure, and adrenaline that Type A males do.

Women are more likely to experience stress as a result of emotional situations as opposed to the kinds of "paper problems" that produce stress in men.

When women experience setbacks, failures, or emotional pressures, they generally respond by expressing or succumbing to depression.

13

MEN AND WOMEN WORKING TOGETHER

In the boardroom or in staff meetings, men deal with objective reality. Men *always* deal with objective reality *first*. They look outside themselves to see what is going on, while women look inside. We've noted earlier that this is not something we are trained to do. Experiments show that from the time we are born, males and females have very distinct ways of perceiving reality.

When the man looks outside himself, his action is often mistakenly interpreted as blame. If something is not working with his staff, he might say, "How did that happen? Who did that?" He will look for one person as the problem. If he can fix that one person, then he can move on. It is the most efficient method of resolution for him.

A woman at the same staff meeting will look inside (subjective) to see what she might have done to contribute to the problem. If she has an insight into the solution, she might volunteer that information. The man's response is likely to be, "Great, then fix it." It appears to the woman as if he is only interested in finding out who to blame; then he can wash his hands of it. From her perspective, he's ignoring the concept of teamwork. What she does not realize is that men don't work as a team in the same way that women do. The male approach to teamwork is that each person has a separate function and that each is independent (exclusive). Men gauge good teamwork by how little the team has to talk to each other (instructions, directions, and so forth). Men easily work side-by-side for long periods of time without saying a word. The female approach is just the opposite: The team has a purpose, and each member is dependent on the other (inclusive). Women gauge good teamwork by how well the team members interact, and communication is a critical factor.

CHILDLIKE GAMES

Researchers conducted an experiment with children and their games and published their findings in *Boys and Girls: Superheros in the Doll Corner.* The children were separated into all-boy and all-girl groups. As in any game, in order to play, rules needed to be identified. The boys and girls made up their rules and began to play.

The Boys

When the researchers observed the little boys, they noted that after playing the game for a while, one of the participants got hurt. His injury was interfering with the game. The other little boys dragged him off the field and continued to play. For them, the game was more important than the individual. So what if he was bleeding? (Sometimes it's fun to bleed! I remember having contests with other boys to see who would bleed first.)

In another instance, the researchers heard one little boy say, "I don't like this rule." The other boys said to him, "Either you play by our rules or get out of the game."

Isn't that how men talk? They set up the rules, and everyone is expected to submit, or they tell you to go start your own team. Again, the game is more important than the needs of the individual.

The Girls

When the researchers observed the little girls playing, they noted that after a while, one of them got hurt. They stopped the game until the little girl was fine. For the girls, the individual player was more important than the game.

Later, one of the little girls said, "Oh, I have a better idea about the rules."

All of the girls discussed her idea, changed some of the rules, and played a new (and to them, better) version of the game.

Our work situations often reflect the "child's play" observed by the researchers.

Men and women get together for a particular purpose. "Okay, we're going to set up this game, and here are the rules for it." All the men and women agree to the rules. After a while, someone gets "hurt." The men say, "Hang in there, we made the rules, don't worry about it, it will work." The women may feel that the men are being inconsiderate, cold, or lacking in compassion.

Then perhaps a woman comes up with a suggestion for a new rule. The men become suspicious. They assume that the woman is being flighty, or they figure that she couldn't really have meant it when she agreed to the rules, because they know a man will keep to the rules until he dies. When a man and woman begin a relationship, they also "agree" on the rules. However, when the woman suggests a change, the man feels he has been trapped and manipulated.

We observed earlier that men and women are usually more at ease with their own genders unless they have been reared in a very dominant opposite-gender household. Men are more at ease with other men because they don't have to remember to be polite, socialized, or conscious of the language they use. Women can be more comfortable with other women because they don't have to be as careful about their language, and they can also relax their constant monitoring of the sexual undertones that seem to be present in mixed-gender conversations. Men can discuss topics of male interest without being accused of being insensitive and talking only about "surface" issues such as sports, or cars, or business. Women can discuss their favorite topics without being accused of "over-emotionalizing" everything, or going into too much detail, or caring too much about the subtleties of relationships.

While male-trained females and female-trained males "feel" more comfortable with the *opposite* sex, they seem to be plagued with a sense of having missed a very important connection in their lives. These individuals find it difficult to relate to the male or female in themselves because that expression was either limited or totally denied to them when they were growing up.

Women are entering the marketplace as business owners in equal numbers with men, and the number of women as chief executive officers, company presidents, and upper-level managers is growing daily. As a result, many attitudinal changes also are emerging, as reported in a 1986 Virginia Slims American Women's Opinion Poll:

1. More *men* than women say they perceive the existence of discrimination in the workplace.
2. Both men and women now report that they prefer a marriage of shared responsibility.
3. Seventy-four percent of employed men now say they'd feel comfortable if their wives made more money than they did.
4. Fifteen years ago, 58% of the men polled said they'd have less respect for a "house husband" who took on the main domestic chores. At the time of the current study, only 25% polled thought "real men" didn't cook (barbecue doesn't count!).

In her book, *The Four-minute Sell,* Janet Elsea examines gender-determined stereotypes and their positive or negative connotations: Being white (in our culture) still carries more authority than being non-white, and being male still means more power and authority than being female. Men are generally rated as more credible by both men and women, even if women have better credentials.

Because nonverbal cues can sometimes alter negative preconceptions regarding race and/or gender identification, nonverbal communication is extremely important. This is especially true when one is attempting to make a favorable first impression on a job interview or with a new client. For instance, there are gender-based differences in eye contact. Women engage in more direct eye contact than men, especially when men are talking. However, women tend to avert their eyes more frequently than men when it's their turn to speak.

THE DISTRACTIVENESS OF ATTRACTIVENESS

According to Elsea, less attractive women actually had a significant edge over their more attractive peers when seeking a place in management. Good looks were an advantage only when women were applying for nonmanagerial positions. Attractiveness also resulted in lower salary recommendations when the women were considered for promotion to an out-of-sex-role position.

These findings imply that women should strive to appear as unattractive and "masculine" as possible if they want to advance to powerful organizational positions.

IDEALIZED WORK PHYSIQUES

Purdue psychologists Kay Deaux and Laurie Lewis found through recent experiments that the expected and ideal male and female body styles—women should be thin, and men should be muscular—influence how people become subject to gender stereotyping. Both men and women who have a body type that is relatively tall, strong, and broad-shouldered are more likely to be seen by others as having masculine personalities and are expected to hold traditionally masculine jobs. Both men and women with a dainty, feminine appearance or a mild-mannered voice were judged to have feminine personalities and jobs.

In addition, they found that grooming was an important factor when considering a woman's management potential. The research seems to hold up the notion that in today's business world, if a woman looks too feminine she may be denied an upper-level management position.

Many of the best-selling dress-for-success books advise women to wear their hair short, use cosmetics sparingly, and wear conservative suits if they want to get ahead in business. Unfortunately, the research suggests that this advice is still relatively sound. (The situation will change as more women take positions of power and influence. Being at the top will allow them to set the standards!)

Except for "love handles," possible baldness, and the size of his sex organ, a man usually gives little attention to his appearance. A man's biggest concern is *how women will perceive him.* He has little or no concern around other men, who could care less about his appearance; in fact, he may even take pride in his disarray.

Men will dress to indicate status, power, or wealth; to exhibit loyalty or authority by wearing uniforms; to declare affiliations; to be appropriate (the right tuxedo); and to be noticeable (the correct jewelry). But a man's sense of ease comes from fitting in with other men—not being over- or under-dressed, but looking exactly as he "should." All the men in the room could be wearing the exact same tuxedo or navy suit and be comfortable. Can you imagine all the women at a social event wearing the exact same dress as all the other women and being comfortable about it? An exception to the variety of women's attire is apparent in very strict, male-dominated cultures or religions where women's attire conforms to male standards. The more individual and cultural freedom a woman has, the more expressive she will be in her choice of fabrics, colors, and style.

DOUBLE-BREASTED BUSINESS STANDARDS

A 1986 study by California Business Magazine of 500 owners and presidents of California businesses revealed that women executives differ substantially from men executives in background, personal convictions, and management styles.

Twice as many female executives as their male counterparts characterized business associates as "less than honest." Two percent said others were "never honest," an opinion shared by none of the men.

Asked if their career was the most important thing in life, 40 percent of the women executives said yes, compared with 28 percent of the men. The women's dedication to their careers also seemed to involve greater personal sacrifice. According to the survey, female business owners and chief executive officers were less likely to be married than men and were more likely to be divorced. Given the choice between attending a child's graduation or an important business meeting, these women were more likely to attend the meeting than the men surveyed.

Such findings confirm what women have known for years: that they have to get up earlier, work harder, and be tougher than men in order to be recognized as successful business people. All individuals or groups who attempt to include themselves in the power base (minority) must go through the process of proving themselves. Sometimes, it takes centuries.

A survey by Peter Dubno, professor of behavioral science and management at the New York University Graduate School of Business Administration, indicates that despite all the feminist gains of the past two decades, male graduate business students feel significantly more negative about women executives than do female graduate students. The responding students were from three graduate schools of business, and the survey was taken in 1975, 1978, and 1983. There was no change over the eight years: The male students' attitudes about women as managers were consistently negative.

All males on some level (conscious or unconscious) are somewhat uncomfortable when dealing with females.

Early wisdom had it that working women must learn to control the traits that are stereotypically labeled "female," since female behavior is what men devalue and tend to deride in themselves. Today we know that for women to try to win men's respect by working harder and longer is futile. The only equality guaranteed in this approach is that women will one day reach men's rate of heart disease. For one thing, women who have made it to the top ranks or have succeeded in a profession are already working hard.

As women adopt men's "workaholic" habits, unsupportive colleagues are unlikely to be impressed by their dedication. So instead of feeling admired and respected for their commitment, these super-hardworking women end up feeling used.

When we recognize and utilize the differences in male and female realities, each gender will be fully appreciated for their contributions to the quality of life on this planet.

ESTABLISHING TEAMS

In one experiment by psychologist Wendy Wood, 90 male and 90 female college students were arranged in gender-segregated groups and were then asked to answer three questions. Half of the groups were told to come up with as many answers as possible, and the other half were told to write down only the best answers the team could devise.

The average all-male group came up with 58 answers in the half-hour allotted, compared with 47 answers from the women. (Men are generally more task-oriented than women, and therefore had an advantage in this experiment.) However, when the researchers analyzed the results of the discussion groups, the answers from the all-women groups were slightly longer, better-presented, and "more creative" than those given by the men's groups. (Women invest a great deal of time in establishing harmony and a sense of involvement among group members.)

The researchers noted that in group work some women tend to be extremely task-oriented, while some men tend to be highly process-oriented. But overall, men are better candidates for brainstorming groups, and women are better candidates for situations when the *quality* of the solution is important.

WHEN MARRIED WOMEN WORK

Recent evidence suggests that when married women are employed, their husbands are often the losers. According to the *American Sociological Review,* a major interview study of American men and women was conducted in 1976 by the University of Michigan's Institute for Social Research. In a resourceful analysis of the national data, sociologists Ronald Kessler and James McRae, Jr. found that although married women who were employed tended to enjoy better mental health than homemakers, the husbands of employed wives tended to have lower self-esteem and more symptoms of depression than husbands of homemakers.

One of the factors in the earnings gaps between men and women results from the "clustering" impact of women in such occupations as secretary, clerk, nurse, etc. These positions are not paid as much as the job categories where men constitute a majority, such as carpenter, painter, electrician, etc., and *The New York Times* reported in 1986 that for each additional percentage point of women employed in a job category, the pay goes down by about $42 a year. In other words, the higher the percentage of, say, librarians who are women, the less librarians as a group will be paid.

THE CONCEPT OF COMPARABLE WORTH

Equal pay for equal work, "comparable worth," may be a difficult idea to sell to women as well as men. In a research study in 1987, psychologist Brenda Major assigned 51 undergraduate men and women to a temporary work project. Each student was told that they would be assigned to a job that had equal demands but was different in that one was usually thought of as a masculine occupation, one a feminine occupation, and one that employed men and women equally. Each student was then told that their pay would be determined by what job they were assigned and how well they performed. The students did not know that each of the jobs was actually identical.

The women believed that they should earn $1.93 for 15 minutes of work no matter which job they were assigned. The men thought that they should earn an average of $2.31. In addition, Major observed that regardless of job assignment or pay received, the women were happier with their situation than the men.

The differences between the attitudes of men and women have interesting implications for the workplace. According to Major and Forcey, men seem to feel more entitled to job benefits than women do. Men are not as grateful as women, nor are they as likely to react to pay incentives or to a chance to be a decision-maker by working harder in return.

Men who considered themselves to be well paid (by their own evaluation) said they put forth more effort than the average person did. However, substantially more well-paid women than men actually put forth extra effort.

In the job market, women demonstrate more commitment and self-sacrifice than men. Professionals and managers are more committed than blue-collar workers, but both groups contain more committed women than men.

Surveys show that women respondents at all levels said they could improve on their work performance more often than their male counterparts. Remember our observation that men are objective and look outside themselves to discover what needs to be fixed, while women look inside themselves to discover what is wrong. Men mistakenly assume that women's looking inside themselves for the problem is a sign of low self-esteem.

Despite such findings, the traditional attitude that a woman's commitment to her job and her family must be mutually exclusive still dominates many industries and regions. A woman who announces marriage plans can still expect to be asked whether or not she will continue to work.

In talking with the women in my workshops, I've discovered that when women marry, their work performance is either unaffected or zooms upward. Women typically have far less trouble handling a change in personal circumstances than their male co-workers and employers. In fact, often a woman's greatest problem is how to manage others' reactions to change, not her own.

From a male perspective, which entails his projecting how he would deal with the responsibility of multiple commitments to career and family, a woman would have to let something slip in order to handle both job and family. The man's exclusive thinking, as opposed to the woman's inclusive thinking, sets him up to expect her to either (a) do a bad job in both aspects of her life, or (b) be forced to give one of them up.

Recent large-scale studies of American values by Philip Blumstien, Ph.D. and Pepper Schwartz, Ph.D., show that women who work outside the home tend to have more power in their relationships at home. This is true not only because working women have money and therefore a greater voice in the "partnership," but also because a man accords his female partner greater respect (and therefore more power) if she earns money. A man's self-respect is significantly derived from his work, and he tends to respect paid employment more than unpaid housework.

SMILING: A GENDER TAG

According to Marian Sandmaier, studies show that women smile a lot more than men. As you and I have observed, not only do they smile more often, but women's smiles tend to be bigger and show more teeth than men. Women smile more at men than they do at other women, and they even smile at men when men don't smile back. Surprisingly, the studies show that women smile even when they're told not to!

Many men interpret a female smile as a sign of genuine interest, usually sexual interest. This assumption puts women in an awkward situation: When she doesn't smile, she risks being called distant or "cold," and if she does smile, she's likely to be called a tease.

The dangers of her smiling aren't just limited to a woman's personal life. Women in professional or managerial positions face an equally confusing problem: how to appropriately express her joy. (Remember, even at birth females smile more than males.) Upper management (modeled by men) expects a woman to project a reserved, business presence. Without being trained otherwise, women may smile during business meetings or while making an important sales presentation. In male/female business interactions, a woman's smile can invite interruptions and is often perceived by men as a sign of submission.

INTEREST VERSUS ABILITY

Both sexes confuse *interest* with *ability*. Men often assume that women can't perform a certain task or shouldn't be asked to participate in a particular event because men don't usually see women engaged in that activity. Men, looking from the physical, practical point of view (if she *could* do it, she *would!*) lose sight of interest as a motivating factor. Women make opposite assumptions: If a man is capable of talking about his emotions, then he should be interested in doing so. If he were capable of occasional spontaneity, then he would be interested in being spontaneous more often.

One example of interest versus ability was revealed in a recent study about computers. More males enjoy computers because of their interest. Males seem to adapt more quickly and easily because of the way the computers operate—not because of a higher aptitude or ability.

A Computer Aptitude, Literacy and Interest Profile (CALIP) test was designed by researchers Mary Poplin, David Drew, and Robert Gale. Their original assumption was that women had less aptitude than men did for computers. The test results from 1,200 people between the ages of twelve and sixty contradicted their assumption. The women approached the problems qualitatively (inclusively), while the men approached the problems quantitatively (exclusively).

Women look at context and interactions (relationships). Women reported that they love computers for what they do, but "wouldn't want to spend the evening with one." Some women refuse to use a computer because they find it inappropriate to their lives, not because they can't master its operation.

Computers are quite objective—a very "black and white" reality. A data bit is either on or off. There is no gray. The computer is the rational person's ideal machine. Based on pure logic, the computer does not deal in attitudes, does not care how quickly or slowly its keys are pressed, and doesn't know whether it's being tapped gently or pounded on. Men are more at ease than women in relating to this "John Wayne" of the mind. It soon becomes a rational, logical, and consistent friend who will only let you down if it is very sick, and even then it has its own diagnostic programs to let you know what's wrong with it. It certainly won't blame you if it gets sick, and it won't expect you to know its heart of hearts. There is no communication between operator and computer, just responses. Even though computers are useful, reliable, and certainly necessary for many jobs, they will never, for a female, resemble a good friend. Women want more relationship, more dialogue, more give and take.

As computers become more animate and are able to delve into the subjective realm (artificial intelligence is still in the future), I predict that women will become more active and enthusiastic users.

SOLVING PROBLEMS

Men use force (energy) to produce results. Physical force includes muscle, armies, and money; and intellectual force includes semantics, rationale, and logic. While women also have the ability to use force, it is emotionally very expensive for them; more often they use the power of intention. In a woman's inclusive process, the desired result may already be known, and the stages through which the result must pass on its way to manifestation are allowed to reveal themselves (discovery versus determination).

Men and women tend to approach problem solving by opposite means, much like a painter and sculptor. The painter starts with a blank canvas and builds the painting. Layer upon layer and section after section are applied. More and more detail is added until the painting is finished (sequential/exclusive). The painting is done when the painter has put the last drop of paint on the canvas and says it is done.

The sculptor, however, "sees" the finished work within the block of marble (asequential/inclusive). The finished work already exists inside, but it needs to be revealed for others to see it. Nothing needs to be added. One hundred percent of the sculpture already exists. Men tend to approach reality as "painters" and women tend to approach reality as "sculptors."

According to what we observed in earlier chapters, men approach problems as follows:

1. Sequential (a, b, c, d, e);
2. Focused (concentrating on one idea at a time);
3. Marked by boundaries (imposing preset rules and regulations).

Women can draw on these same qualities, but they have the added advantage of being able to approach problems

1. Asequentially (using random information and ideas without the slow process of sequencing);
2. In an unfocused way (being able to handle more than one idea at a time and actually being able to deal with two or more problems simultaneously);
3. Without imposing boundaries (ignoring preset rules and regulations, real or imagined).

Men also have the ability to use these "feminine" processes, but they use them much less often and with much more difficulty than women do.

During my corporate workshops, I divide the room into separate gender groups. I then assign problems for them to solve and ask them to track how they achieve their results. During follow-up discussions, the different approaches to problem solving are clear-cut.

MALE AND FEMALE HUMOR

Men and women differ distinctly in their use and appreciation of humor. Most of us are all too aware that the opposite sex doesn't necessarily find the same things to be funny that we do.

Distinctions appear in male/female humor as early as the preschool years. According to child studies, the comprehension and appreciation of humor is generally equal among boys and girls, with one very significant difference: Boys enjoy and pursue hostile humor.

Beginning at ages four or five, they are more likely than girls to choose aggressive cartoons as funnier, and the humor they initiate during play tends to be more hostile than that of girls. Throughout grade school, boys indulge in more silly rhymes, naughty words, and teasing than girls.

In an office environment, humor is used by men as a very strong bonding and team-building technique. It is a comfortable way for men to relieve stress and to let down their guard. Men usually find great joy in practical jokes. If one of the team goes on vacation, he can be sure he'll return to some prank the others have waiting for him. The joke could be that someone has rearranged his desk or that all the drawers are reversed or locked. While this type of humor may appear demeaning to women, it actually demonstrates that the male team members admire their buddy enough to spend time and energy making up these pranks. It is similar to aggressive play among boys, and to the horseplay among men in beer commercials. Its purpose is not just to vent aggression, but to indicate that someone belongs. It's a way for men to comfortably express how they feel toward other men and women.

A joke or a slap on the back intended as a positive message can sometimes be interpreted as an outrageous insult by women, especially those who did not grow up with brothers. These insults, or "ranking," (the art of competitive, humorous insulting) are a favorite pastime of men. The "roasts" men conduct at meetings actually honor the person being roasted, even though the comments may be derogatory. Through the use of jokes and humor, men develop team spirit without having to put emotions into words. Men instinctually know that if a man can be teased about his body, his style, and his attitude, and laugh about it, he must have a strong self-image. He can be trusted.

While humor builds comradery with men and is an important tool for making men comfortable, the effective use of humor can also ease relationship tensions and indicate that a woman is in control. Humor helps define and distinguish the power structure in a group.

Any woman who can interact comfortably and easily with the aggressive humor of men in business is one step ahead of the woman who negatively interprets these interactions. Obviously, this does not imply that women or men should put up with deliberate insults, chauvinistic attitudes, or racist remarks for the sake of being on the team.

The most disconcerting thing a woman can do is to take a humorous comment personally or seriously, yet that is often a woman's reaction. It is not easy to stay poised and appear confident when you're the target of a put-down or a joking attack, but unless you can respond with something witty or funny, you're in deep trouble, and the situation will probably be awkward for everybody. By responding with an appropriate comeback, a woman restores the balance of power between herself and the man who made the joke at her expense. By misinterpreting the situation as a personal attack, women sometimes respond with a personal attack that the man genuinely does not understand.

Sometimes, a woman may feel compelled to defend a member of the team who is being joked about, when in actuality, the person may be enjoying the attention and its accompanying sign of acceptance. Most men have learned to be cautious about using humor with women because they can't be sure how women will respond. But they try, nonetheless.

One study by sociologist Rose Laub Coser showed that both sexes find it funnier when a woman is the butt of a joke. *Self-ridicule* (subjective reality) is the basis of most humor used by women. Because of her introspection, the use of self-depreciation may be one of the most significant differences between how men and women use humor.

In a 1976 study by Zillmann and S. Holly Stocking, men consistently rated self-disparagers significantly less confident, less intelligent, and less witty than the person who puts down a friend or enemy. Women consistently showed a more favorable attitude toward the self-disparager, regardless of gender, than men did. One common motive for self-disparaging is that when a mistake or deficiency can't be ignored, pointing it out yourself denies others the opportunity to do so and, in the end often serves to save face. But anyone who wants to be regarded as a leader will avoid self-ridicule.

Although men are usually the initiators of jokes, women who know their co-workers' style of humor can take the lead and gain a valuable advantage. Humor wielded wisely and well is a less obvious intrusion into traditional masculinity than more direct expressions of dominance and aggression. Humor is a tactic women can and should use often. In fact, the ability to make and take a joke might be one of the most important on-the-job skills a woman can develop in working with men.

BALANCE OF TRADE

There's a fundamental male characteristic that can be utilized when dealing with men: They always work on trade. They trade for everything, and everything is negotiable, whether it appears to be or not. A man is always keeping track of who owes whom. On a conscious or unconscious level, there is always a list.

For example, if I were watching a football game and another man were sitting next to me, and I said, "Hey, we're out of beer," do you know what happens? Nothing! Nobody moves. Nobody gets up. Nobody runs to the kitchen—*unless one of the other guys owes me.* It could be that we had a bet on the last play, or that it's his turn to go, or that he's the host, or that we have some type of agreement, but then and only then will someone get the beer.

On the other hand, if a woman and I are watching television and I say, "Hey, we're out of beer," she gets up and gets the beer to make me happy. I start to expect that. I can say "Hey, we're out of beer," and the beer appears. (After about two or three years into the relationship, she says "I'm not your - - - slave," or something like that.) But as a man, I wouldn't have gotten up and gotten the beer unless I wanted to, so I assumed she wanted to, or that she owed me, or why did she bother getting up? To please me? Because she loves me? Sure, but what's in it for her? There has to be something, or she wouldn't do it (so men assume!). This may sound very cold and rational, but it's actually how men make "logical" deductions. When I discuss this example with women, some of them say that when I said, "Hey, we're out of beer," what they heard was, "Hey, get me a beer."

In most household situations, women think they have to resolve the problems alone. A woman's conversation might sound like this: "You're going to work, and I want to go to work, but if I don't get a cleaning person, then I have to do it all myself."

Consider: The woman is assuming responsibility for the housework. If she were as willing to have the house be as dirty as he's willing to have it, then it wouldn't be such a big issue. But her standards are higher, her needs different, and so the dirt annoys her sooner. He thinks the house or apartment is comfortable.

If women don't want sole responsibility for the housework, then the problem needs to be communicated differently. For example, a woman could say, "I'm going to work on Monday, you're going to work on Monday, and *we* don't have someone to clean the house. What are *we* going to do?" (Now, it's *we* who have the problem, not just the woman.) If the man doesn't volunteer to help, it's probably because he believes she owes him and that he doesn't have to get involved with this particular problem. This is a good way to find out what's on his list. He will say, "Well, I'm doing this, I'm doing this, and I'm doing this." (Remember, a man doesn't know when a woman is serious, so if his first response is "no," he may be checking to see if she really means it.)

In order for a man to do something (pick up around the house, for instance), there has to be something in it for him—some kind of treat (reason). The size of the request (assuming the relationship is in balance) determines the size of the reward. That system always works. Men may not know it, but unconsciously, they're keeping score all the time. This sounds analytical, rational, and demeaning, but to another man, it's an easy way for him to know who is doing what to whom. It makes life very simple. So if she says, "Take out the garbage," and he says, "Why?" she could say, "Well, for the last three days, I've done this, this, and this." He'll say, "Okay, I'll get up and take the garbage out." If he doesn't, then he is telling her that he thinks she still owes him something, that he thinks he is doing more than she is, or that he feels he isn't being appreciated for something. This is a good opportunity for them to sit down and evaluate what's on each person's list.

If the woman earns more money, she can use that fact in the negotiation. If the woman earns less, then the man probably assumes his larger paycheck buys him a certain number of "non-trips" to empty the garbage! There is always an equivalency, a trade.

Given the fact that women don't bother keeping track of debts in the same way men do, they don't bother to remind men of all they do. If a woman puts her list up against the man's, he will probably back off. If he doesn't, he still has some items on his list, or he doesn't trust her.

To resolve some of these issues is to find out what the man thinks he has on his list. Ask a man, "Who owes whom here?" or "Whose turn is it?" and he'll tell you. He knows, at all times, who is in what position. It's automatic for him. So when men are with other men, they know whose turn it is to buy. If they forget, it's all right to tease, argue, and fight over it. Women regard this behavior as macho, competitive, and childish, but it is an essential part of male balance.

There is an economic fact of life every working woman faces: She earns roughly 70 cents for every dollar a man earns, yet women make up 42.4 percent of the work force. (These figures vary according to who is doing the survey, but the range is between 65-75 cents.) The business world no longer needs to be trained to accept women. Rather, what is needed is an understanding and appreciation of a work force whose biggest contribution can be made by *not* fitting into the male role model.

Most companies are in desperate need of safe opportunities for men and women to discuss issues as perceived from each point of view or "reality." Open forums are an excellent way to take an intelligent and compassionate look at the needs of everyone on the team. The combined attributes of males and females can be an unbeatable asset on the balance sheet of any family, company, community, or country.

CHAPTER SUMMARY

Men always deal with objective reality first.

The male approach to teamwork is that each person has a separate, independent function (exclusive), and the game is more important than its individual participants.

Men gauge good teamwork by how little the team members have to talk to each other.

The female approach to teamwork is that the team has a purpose and each member is dependent on the other (inclusive); the individual participant is more important than the game, and communication is a critical factor.

Men and women are usually more at ease with their own gender unless they have been reared in a very dominant opposite-gender household.

Men are generally rated as more credible by both men and women, even if women have better credentials.

Nonverbal communication can sometimes alter negative preconceptions regarding race and/or gender identification.

When seeking a place in management, less attractive women actually had a significant edge over their more attractive peers.

The differing idealized physiques—thin for women, muscular for men—influence gender stereotyping in the workplace.

The more freedom a woman has, the more expressive she will be in her choice of fabrics, colors, and style.

All individuals or groups who attempt to include themselves in the power base must go through the process of proving themselves.

Overall, men make better candidates for brainstorming groups, and women make better candidates when the *quality* of the solution is important.

One of the factors contributing to earnings gaps is a result of discrimination against the "clustering" of women in certain occupations.

Comparable worth is a tough idea to sell, especially since many women still don't believe their work is worth as much as men's.

Professionals and managers are more committed to their work than blue-collar workers, but in both groups, there are more committed women than men.

When women marry, their work performance is either unaffected or zooms upward.

A woman's greatest problem is often to manage others' reactions to change, not her own.

Women who work outside the home tend to have more power in their relationships at home.

A man's self-respect is significantly derived from his work, and he tends to respect paid employment more than housework.

Women smile more than men, and in business interactions, a smile may invite interruptions and is often seen as a sign of submission.

Women are more likely to approach problems qualitatively (inclusively), while men prefer quantitative measurements (exclusive).

Men use force (energy) to produce results.

Women have the ability to use force, or they can use the power of intention.

Men approach problems:
- sequentially (a, b, c, d, e);
- in a focused way (using one idea at a time);
- by imposing limitations (preset rules and regulations).

Women can approach problems in the same manner as men, but have the added advantage of being able to approach problems
- asequentially (using random information and ideas without the slow process of sequencing);

- in an unfocused way (being able to handle more than one idea at a time and actually being able to deal with two or more problems simultaneously);
- without imposing limitations (ignoring preset rules and regulations, real or imagined).

Through jokes and humor, men develop team spirit without having to put any emotions into words.

Women who interact comfortably and easily with the aggressive humor of men in business are far likelier to succeed than women who negatively interpret male humor.

Both sexes find it funnier when a woman is the butt of a joke.

Self-disparagement may be one of the most significant differences between the humor of men and women.

Anyone who wants to be regarded as a leader will avoid self-ridicule.

The ability to make and take a joke may be one of the most important on-the-job skills a woman can cultivate.

Trade is an effective technique to use with men.

Women can make their biggest contribution to the work force by not fitting into the male role model.

The combined attributes of males and females is an unbeatable asset.

14

OPEN DIALOGUE

While you've been reading this book, many questions may have popped into your mind. In my workshops, participants have an opportunity to ask their favorites, and they are included here as examples.

ANSWERS TO COMMON QUESTIONS FROM MEN AND WOMEN

Male question: "Why are women so manipulative?"

Your question demonstrates part of our difficulty in conversation between men and women. First, your question makes an assumption that "women are manipulative." Secondly, it assumes a negative connotation to the word "manipulative," and thirdly, it assumes that men and women would agree on the definition of the word.

If you put male standards on how women should behave, then women appear manipulative. Men are very simple. They're not very complicated. They're not very sophisticated in the way they approach things. So when it looks like women are making too much out of a little thing that really isn't going on, the fact is, it is going on, and men don't see it.

Female question: "I don't relate very well with women. Is this because I was taught by men and have adopted some of their rules in order to get along in their world?"

The discomfort between you and other women is probably because you're "acting male" without realizing it. Women will respond to you as they would to a male and automatically and instinctively separate themselves from you. Their question is, "How can I trust you if you are operating in a way that is different from me?"

The men around you let you be one of the boys, or they let you play their games, or they let you have the job, because you learned to negotiate at that level. When you are with women (or others) who don't negotiate or don't understand the process of negotiating the "male way," their reaction is likely to be, "Why should I be around you? Your way of being is so much like a man's that I might as well be around one of them."

Female question: "Why are men such babies when they're hurt or sick?"

Because when it does hurt, it's surprising. Suddenly, we are smacked in the face by our physical limitations, and therefore feel very vulnerable. A wounded animal is easy prey. When men are hurt or sick, they seek protection, because during the recovery period, all their energy is expended on healing.

I also believe that males, on a very unconscious level, are always particularly aware of their mortality. More male babies are spontaneously aborted, more males than females die of childhood disorders in the first two years, and men still die eight years younger than women.

Female question: "How do we set up neutral territory and create an atmosphere where we are not constantly 'stepping' on one another?"

First, know that you *are* going to constantly step on each other! Don't take it personally! It happens in all relationships.

Second, when the emotions are running high, don't discuss whatever it is you need to discuss when you're in the middle of the event. If the issue is about sex, don't discuss it in bed; discuss it at the kitchen table when the pressure is off. If it's about moving, don't talk about it while you're lifting something. If it's about jobs and career, don't try to solve it while you're working on the checkbook. Get yourself out of the immediate environment of whatever it is that you're dealing with. Later, you can say, "Can we talk about this? This is something I think we need to talk about." Look at his "balance sheet" to see what he needs. Then look at yours to see what you need. If you're putting up with an environment that's unhealthy, you're starting out behind. And if you don't realize you're drained when you start the negotiation, you're going to be in trouble.

Obviously, the most important thing is to listen as if the other person is telling you the truth, whether or not it makes sense to you. And ask them to listen to you in the same way. Establish a time when you both agree to talk, and if that's not possible, you might want to consider talking to a professional therapist or counselor specializing in relationships.

Male question: "Women are more insecure than men, and it seems they have to have a man in their lives, or they don't feel 'full.' Why is that?"

Watch out for "charged" words like *insecure*. What you call insecure may be an attempt by women to be comfortable and have their needs met. Men are seeking the same satisfaction, but they express it differently.

It's a fact that men and women are healthier and live longer in harmonious relationships. Men interpret insecure as meaning that women *have* to be in a relationship, as opposed to understanding what women are actually seeking. Women cultivate relationships as a place for them to express, where they can be themselves, where they can relax, where they don't have to worry about sexuality, where they don't have to worry about contracting diseases, where they don't have to worry about pregnancy, and so forth. A lot more is involved than simply, "I need a man."

The average American male is 5'10" and weighs 170 pounds; the average American women is 5'4" and weighs 130 pounds. A man takes a lot of things for granted that women have to deal with every day, but he thinks, "What's the big deal?" Yet there are very few doors too heavy for him, and there's hardly any alley too dark. Men can take care of themselves in the physical universe without incurring the "overhead" that women constantly amass.

If you assume something that may or may not be true, such as, "I know you're insecure about relationships," then there is no communication. You've already made your decision. You've already stopped listening. You've made a decision, and there's no place the relationship can go.

Granted, there are some insecure men and some insecure women. Not everyone is in wonderful, healthy shape. We are still evolving. We're still in process.

Male question: "Why are women so weird when it comes to cards and gifts?"

Even today's most understanding men **do not begin to understand how much more presents mean to women than they do to men.** Certain holidays, like birthdays or Valentine's Day (and especially no occasion at all) have emotional significance to women that men don't feel or relate to.

Contrary to men's assumptions, the size of the gift is not important. Men are slow to realize the significance a woman will attach to (or read into) a gift from a man. As a result, men give gifts that deliver all kinds of signals they never intended to send.

Women assume that all aspects of the gift were considered. Many women read men's gifts as if the gift were an interesting mystery—every element a clue, every nuance a revelation, as if it came with all the elements of subtlety that a woman might bring to gift-giving. As a result, women sometimes feel a lack of romanticism in men's gifts where there is only a lack of understanding; or they experience disappointment at the lack of "feeling" that went into the choice where there was only a lack of thought. The point is that women decipher gift messages with a woman's code book, not a man's.

Male comment: "You talk about men being more aggressive and willing to fight on a moment's notice. I wouldn't even think of fighting with you. I'm not a conflict type of person. I'm not aggressive. I don't even think of getting in fights. I think that's annoying, even disgusting."

Yes, I agree with you. But if you were walking out of this room and I was walking into the room and there was only enough space for one of us to pass through the door and I happened to hit your shoulder, what's the first thing you would think of?

"Well, not to fight, of course!"

But one can only choose "not to fight" after the instinct "to fight" is evaluated. Obviously you decided not to, but the chemistry in your body is automatic. That same chemistry doesn't exist in a woman's body. It's not even an issue.

I would hope that we can eliminate fighting, weapons, and wars as solutions. But on the other hand, I need to know that my body is able to respond to those conditions. For men, there's always the *potential* for conflict. What we do about potential conflict depends on our intelligence, sophistication, socialization, and the severity of the circumstances.

Male question: "Why are women such lousy drivers?"

Statistics actually show that men are about twice as likely as women to break the law while driving. Market researchers at R. H. Bruskin Associates surveyed 1,000 adults about their driving experiences in 1985, and the survey showed that 63% of the men—but only 40% of the women—had at some time been in an accident while behind the wheel. Additional statistics:

Received ticket or summons: 20% men; 10% women

Fined for speeding: 10% men; 5% women

Ticketed for illegal parking: 9% men; 5% women.

While driving a car, women have a "sense" or "experience" of their destination and are engaged in the *process* of getting there. They are not as concerned as men about getting there on time, the number of miles, or the number of minutes involved in the trip.

Women have been accused of being "lousy" drivers because of men's perceptions of the "right" way to drive. And since men need to focus on one thing at a time, they *would* be in trouble if they drove like women!

Female question: "Why does a man stay in a relationship that's dead rather than change?"

The relationship might look dead to you because there's no interaction and no communication, but the man may interpret it differently. To him, there's no noise, there's no bother, there's nobody nagging him to do things that he doesn't want to do.

Men are usually insensitive to subtle messages. A man may be thinking, "Oh, good! She's not making noise or complaining. Things must be better, or she's working it out on her own.'' So what looks dead to you might be a relief to him.

Female question: "Our company president surrounded himself with inferior men, and I watched him gradually get rid of all the 'brains' in the company. Why would he do that?"

It sounds as if he wanted to maintain control, or he didn't want to keep fighting all the time, or he didn't want someone stealing his job. He wanted people who would not compete with him. It's a smart thing to do if that's your point of view. But if a company president wants to expand a company, then he or she looks for people who are more talented than they, and for people who are going to question or confront things to make the plan work.

Male participant: "Why are women so addicted to diets? They always seem to have their attention on their bodies."

Research shows that women perceive their bodies to be about 25% larger than they really are, and they seem to have a constant battle with their physical appearance. I suggest this is because of women's discomfort with physical reality. Women, being inclusive, can experientially go beyond physical limits more easily than men. The body, however, represents an unwitting reminder to a woman that she is bound by a physical limitation.

Body weight has been discussed in almost every group of women that I have worked with. Men have never brought up the subject, except to talk about women's seeming obsession with their weight.

In listening to the women in my workshops, I discovered that they tend to have one of three beliefs about their weight:

1. They believe they are very overweight and need to lose excess poundage (to firm up in different places, get rid of cellulite, and so forth);
2. They believe they are too skinny and need to add curves (but only in specific regions!);
3. They believe they are just right, but need to monitor their weight all the time to make sure they don't become overweight or underweight.

In one workshop, a woman said she was constantly overweight and had to do battle with herself or she would "blimp out." There was a cry of disbelief in the room, because this woman had a body that most of the women would have gladly exchanged for theirs. One woman asked her how she could possibly say that about herself.

"Are you kidding?" she responded. "If I'm not careful, I could gain two pounds in no time at all!" There was another groan. (Most women profess to gain two pounds just walking past the bakery.)

The point here is the woman's personal perspective. To her, that two pounds might as well mean she was twenty or thirty pounds overweight. And despite the groans of jealousy or frustration from the women's group, every woman in the room could relate to that feeling of needing to work on herself.

Female question: "Is it a positive thing for a man to communicate at the mulling level? Or is it just up to women to recognize that mulling is there and that we need to wait until men are ready to communicate?"

The answer is yes to both. Men don't want to emote for the sake of communication. A man's eyes may water up a little bit, and another man might say, "Boy, the guy's really in the middle of it; the guy's in trouble." The man could be fully expressing (for him), and the woman says, "Come on, let it out." Well, *he* is out! This is as far as he wants to go. He's at the edge of his comfort zone and has said everything he needs to say.

Sometimes men could "come out sooner," and sometimes it's unhealthy for them to come out before they're ready. It's just a matter of women knowing the individual man well enough—his style—to know when they're about to "stuff" it. If he says, "No, I'm not ready to talk about it yet," and you know you can trust him, then leaving him alone is a very loving thing to do. It probably will accelerate his processing. What I've discovered is if women say, "Great. Go ahead and keep working on that," then within a short while, he will have finished. He has been empowered by you. He can then come back to you and say, "You know the thing you asked me about?" and he'll be able to talk about it. But it may take a while, especially if he's used to not having to communicate; or if there are other major things in your relationship which have not been resolved.

Female question: "I have a hard time with my husband when he says, 'Don't you want to work?' as if it would be the worst thing in the world if I didn't work. I like working, but I've

done it for quite a few years and now I want to change. Why is he resisting?"

One statistic shows that men commit suicide more often from losing their jobs than from losing their families. It may *look* to him like he gives up as much for his job as you do, but it may not be true.

His job is very important to him; it's part of his expression, part of his emotional release, part of who he is. He's getting some rewards from his job that you aren't getting. He may be having a wonderful time while he's struggling, and you may be tolerating work in order to have some of the things the job produces. But neither of you may realize what it "costs" the relationship to have you do something you really don't want to do.

Female question: "Where do we draw the line on compromises with men?"

A woman in a previous workshop told us her husband insisted on dark brown drapes all through the house. They made it so dark that no plants could grow, but she complied with his wishes so he could be comfortable and relaxed at home. She, however, was not in a healthy state of mind. There was no expression in that "home" for her. Remember, men were built to live in caves and are actually more comfortable in the dark. But they can adjust to light and air and grass more easily than women can adjust to the suppression of a cave. I suggest we would still be living in caves if women hadn't said, "There're too many bones in here, and I don't like the smell of these hides."

Each of us needs to have his or her needs met, and that process consists of identifying, communicating, and then pursuing what we want. If someone loses as the result of another's gain, there is no progress for either. Listen to yourself and begin to recognize that point beyond which you will not go. Most people sacrifice themselves in the name of saving the relationship for themselves, their children, or to avoid community pressure. But thinking it through usually will produce another kind of perspective.

Female question: "My husband is an accountant, and we both work out of the house. But I can't even walk through a room at home without tripping on his papers. I nag him, and I

know I'm not going to score any points this way, but I don't know how to change.''

This has to do with trade and negotiation. Women have a lot of things they give away for free. Men don't—they keep track of all of it. So rather than nag, you could say, ''The house does not function properly with all these papers. I would like another arrangement. We have a problem, but I know we can work it out. What do you see as some possible solutions?''

Female question: ''Men don't seem to fulfill promises—and I don't mean large ones. They say 'yes' to things they're never going to do. If I say I'm going to do something, it's done. Why does this happen?''

This also has to do with negotiation. If there is no cost to him for not doing what he says he will do, it puts you in the role of manager, monitor, or nagger all the time. Most women don't ''charge'' for undelivered promises, so the man discovers he can placate you with a ''yes,'' that you'll then leave him alone, and that you're not going to bother him if he doesn't fulfill his promise. Why should he? It's costing you energy, not him. Also, since sometimes, as a woman, you express to express, the man is confused about whether you really meant for him to keep his promise or just wanted to communicate. Without a consequence or trade, he assumes it was just ''express to express.''

Male question: ''In attempting to communicate in a non-defensive manner, how do we keep things from grinding to a halt? I mean, I can't analyze what she's going to think every time I try to say something.''

This is something men try to figure out in advance—what do I do to avoid a problem?—rather than asking her about it. We hardly ever ask somebody else what they need or want. Those of you who are successful in your negotiations and relationships with people ask, ''What do you need?'' rather than trying in advance to second-guess and being wrong. Instead, we ask ourselves, ''How do I prepare myself to avoid the problem?'' as opposed to asking the other person, ''What did I do wrong? What would you like me to do?'' The risk to the asker is that when the opposite sex says what they would like us to do, it's probably something we don't want to do. Or their answer confuses us or doesn't seem to relate to our question, so we tend not to ask.

An example of "What do you need?" might start when she says, "Well, I just need a hug." What a man would do when she says that is to start calculating. How long should the hug be? If he doesn't hug long enough, it's a waste. If it's a four-minute hug she needs, and he only hugs for three minutes, she might say, "Is that it? Don't you really love me? Where are you going?" If he hugs for too long, it starts to imply something she doesn't want. So he tries to second-guess. If he asks her how long a hug she needs, she'll be insulted. If he says, "Is this a four-minute hug or a three-minute hug?" he's going to have a fight.

But if a *man* says, "I just need some time to be alone," I could say, "How long?" and he could tell me. "Eight minutes." The man would come up with a number and then make it work. He'll force it to be eight minutes—he'll make it happen. If I asked a woman how much time she needed, she would probably say, "I don't know," or "Just a few minutes."

To a man, "just a few minutes" can mean anything from twelve seconds to an hour and a half. In the meantime, the man would look back at his scars and say, "God, the last time a woman said that to me, I had to hang around and do nothing for an hour waiting for her." That's how we get angry at something that wasn't intended as anger-producing.

So we assume we know what's going on with the other person and that we can find out for ourselves without asking them. When we have asked and they've told us, and then we don't want to do that or we don't believe them, then we stop asking and then we get ourselves into trouble. Women do the same thing. They assume they know what men want.

While these questions are typical of what women and men want to know about each other, they also demonstrate just how much we assume about one another and how seldom we acknowledge the actual differences between the sexes. It's been my experience that relationships become a great deal easier and more fulfilling once those differences are taken into account.

15

TECHNIQUES TO BRIDGE THE GENDER GAP

Information is of little value in our lives unless we can apply it to our everyday situations. Here are some suggested techniques which you can put to use immediately. You will discover techniques of your own as you work with these new ideas.

TECHNIQUES

How to empower a woman, even if you don't understand her communication:

There is some behavior men can relate to with women and other behavior that mystifies them no matter how hard they try to understand it. If you are a man and find yourself in one of those situations with a woman, just say, "I have no reality about that at all. I can't even comprehend what you're talking about, but I love you," or "I trust you," or "I respect what you're saying, and I don't need to understand it, and we'll just let it go at that," rather than struggling to find out what it is the woman is saying.

How to get a man involved in seeking solutions:

Men and women simultaneously misidentify intentions. Women tend to say, "I must be misreading this situation. What can I do to fix this?" Keep in mind that the man is involved in the process too. He is also responsible, and you need to hold him accountable for listening to you as you're trying to listen to him. Elicit an understanding between the two of you. The man has to work as hard to meet you halfway as you are working to meet him. Many women become so involved in solving problems that they tend to internalize the problem and then say, "Oh, I see where I did that," and then to start fixing themselves. Naturally, a man's response to this process of hers will be, "Good, you found out what was going wrong and why we had fights. Then fix that, and we won't fight anymore." Instead, allow him to see what he's doing that contributes to the problem; it's a fifty/fifty proposition.

How men (and women) can get out of assumption arguments:

In order for this technique to work, the man has to be willing to give up his own suspicions and trust whatever the woman says.

1. He asks: "Are you angry?" (or whatever he thinks the emotion is). If she says, "No, I'm not," then he should leave it alone. Drop it. If she says, "Yes," then he may go to the next question, which should be asked purely for the man's peace of mind.

2. "Does it have to do with me?" Most of the time, the woman will be surprised that the man assumes he did something to cause the problem, that he thinks everything has to do with him. (Remember, men's exclusive reality has him at the center of everything.) Nine out of ten times she will say, "No, it has nothing to do with you." But even if she says, "Yes, it has to do with you," it is not necessarily a problem for a woman to have a problem with you. She knows that in the process of day-to-day living it probably will get worked out. So for the nine-out-of-ten times that it has nothing to do with the man, he can now be objective and supportive, not defensive. Then he can ask:

3. "Is there something I can do for you?" The man should not ask this question unless he is really willing to do whatever she asks. This will usually be a simple request for a hug, or for some

conversation, or it could be a request for some environmental change. His job now is to be compassionate and supportive.

This technique works equally well with a woman interacting with a man. The woman needs to be able to listen to a man's way of speaking without accusing him of being "too objective and cold-hearted."

How to get a man back in control:

(This technique works for men or for women managing men.)

When a man is given a number of options without enough information to make a clear decision, he may become confused and disoriented. If he appears stopped and out of control:

1. "Fake" certainty. Show signs of being in control. Show very little emotion; keep your breathing slow and steady; show an air of authority.
2. Develop a linear process, so that he can follow your thinking.
3. Ask him to trust you.
4. If he says he can't trust you, ask him what you need to do so he can begin to trust you.
5. In general, when dealing with highly-charged emotional issues, give commands and directions.

A PERSONAL NOTE

Male participant: "I have a very comfortable, yet unsettled feeling. I know there is new information to look into, but it's unsettling. I was wondering, when you delved into this for yourself, what feelings did you get?"

That's a very good question. When I started putting this material together, like anything else we work on, we work on it because we need it, not because the world needs it. I was confused, trying to figure out what was happening in my personal and business relationships with women. In developing the material, the first thing I discovered and had to admit was, "Oh my God, we're in more trouble than I thought. There are more differences between men and women than I could ever have imagined. How are we ever going to get along?"

Then there was a stage of anger. What I found in some of that anger was my frustration at not being understood by women. I was also disappointed and angry at myself because I hadn't always been available to listen when women had been telling me their truth. After a while, my ability to be compassionate returned, but it took some time.

First, I had to deal with the internal anger for having allowed myself to be suppressed at times. I had allowed myself to give in to women. I would say, "Yes, I'll do that," when what I really meant was, "No, I don't want to do that," or "I don't want to go on the shopping trip," or "I don't want to spend this money." I had behaved in ways that demeaned me. I was angry at myself and at the women in my life for having "done that to me."

Then I realized that women weren't deliberately acting in ways to annoy me; in fact, they were actually trying to please me most of those times. I realized that I had misinterpreted women's intentions. Then some more of my anger dissipated.

I also began to develop compassion for myself by knowing that I wasn't deliberately inconsiderate in my behavior toward women, our misunderstandings and hurt feelings were something that just happened in the process of men and women interacting with each other. And then, over time, I was able to be more attentive in conversations with females. I was able to stop myself from giving the automatic male response that I would give to another man. I realized that some of my anger had been automatic, just because it was a woman I was dealing with. I began to ask more questions, such as, "What do you mean by that?" or "How do you feel?" and I learned to say, "I'm sorry" more often. What I found was that some people are unwilling to hear "I'm sorry." They are so angry in their own process that when I said, "I didn't mean that to be an insult. I'm sorry if that insulted you," they said, "Well, - - - it, you should know that's an insult!" I start to withdraw from that type of person. I don't allow myself not to be heard.

Eventually, I released my anger in positive, healthy ways. A male buddy went through some of that process with me. He was available for me, just man-to-man. He could take a punch. He knew, as a man, what it meant for me to be able to "release" with him, and I didn't do it in a nice, polite way. Afterward, we cleaned up whatever we had to clean up so that our relationship wasn't damaged.

My women friends were sympathetic, supportive, and compassionate during most of this. I could emotionally release with them. But it was nice to be with my male friends and not be concerned about getting physically hurt or embarrassed by my behavior.

There is a slow uncovering process which leads to the discovery stage. As I learned more about myself and women, I found myself saying, "Oh, that explains that fight. Now I understand why that happened." Some people experience release from anger in their dreams, or they find themselves behaving differently at work. It's amazing how much cooperation begins to surface from both men and women when we understand and respect one another's reality.

I encourage people to trust themselves more, and I think there is a natural gift of balance when we trust *each other*. What we have are individual gifts to give to the world, to one another, and to our relationships. To look at what we can fix in ourselves and still be "male" or "female" is very healthy exploration.

I believe that all males experience an unconscious feeling of declining usefulness on the planet. More and more of these functions of the male are being replaced by machines, and more and more of the functions will start to be replaced by women. In the past, the survival of the community unit (hunting and food-gathering) was a male's primary function. With the advent of new crops, new ways of processing protein sources, and by raising fish in hatcheries, men's hunting skills (speed and agility; ability to focus on targets) are no longer needed. With the invention of hydraulic equipment, man's brute strength and his ability to withstand pain are no longer necessary. The computer is fast replacing man's rational side: his logical thinking, his sequential methodology, his ability to order and keep track of details. The only reason remaining for man's existence on the planet is procreation, and when cloning has been perfected, even the male's function as sperm donor will disappear. Women will then be the necessary component for the survival and continuation of the human species.

I am not suggesting that these thoughts of male extinction are a conscious part of men's thinking. I am suggesting, however, that men are confused regarding women, and that the underlying cause is their uncertain role, their reason for being in women's lives. Even if the biological material sometimes seems far-fetched as an explanation, I have found that it serves as a powerful metaphor to alleviate our conflicts and set us on the road to congenial relationships.

In one of my workshops, a man began talking about his relationship with his wife. He said he always felt a little unsure of the relationship. He loved her and wanted to be with her for the rest of his life, but he felt a sense of uneasiness that he couldn't put his finger on. After struggling with this realization for a few minutes, he began to cry. (Crying by men in workshops is not rare, but it is unusual enough that it gets everyone's attention.) When we pursued the question, he said he was afraid his wife would leave because he didn't understand why she was with him in the first place. He knew she loved him, but there was an intangible part of her that he felt he could never reach. A nagging little piece of his mind had him wondering about the stability of the relationship since he could not contain the "whole" of it. He knew she was "holding" the relationship, but he couldn't; and he was afraid that if she let go, the relationship would deteriorate and there would be nothing he could do about it.

I was surprised at his insight and thrilled with his openness and his direct honesty. He was not trying to fit his words into any preconceived ideas about relationships, or into any models of how they might or should be. I asked the other men in the room how they felt about what had just been revealed. *All* the men said that they had never verbalized that feeling before, but that it was also true for them. The wives in the room were surprised at the tenderness of their husbands and deeply appreciated the vulnerability that their husbands must have felt. The wives began to see how the husbands were viewing their relationships; how the men depended on them to maintain stability; and how much the men needed reassurances that the relationship was in good shape. I frequently use this example in men's groups, and the participants always validate the experience of uncertainty regarding their relationships and the role they play in them.

I suggest that men need to reinforce their "brotherhoods" and women their "sisterhoods" to provide some feedback and support that both have mistakenly gone to the opposite sex to get. Those gender needs can get taken care of and put back in balance. Then, when we are with the opposite sex, we have the strength to say, "What can I do for you now?" (And we can do it with pleasure and in a healthy way.)

At this point in my life, I find that I have relationships with many kinds of people. I know that there are styles of women I like and styles of women I don't like. There are also styles of men I like and styles of men I don't like. I select friends who are real friends to me. That means that they take the good times with the bad. I surround myself with people who can hear my needs, who are willing to communicate what their needs are, and who are willing to have me be me. That's the basis of my relationships and friendships. I suggest that it be the foundation for yours.

BIBLIOGRAPHY

Benbow, C. "John Hopkins Study of Mathematically Precocious Youth,"
Report to the American Association for the Advancement of Science, Iowa
State Ames, Iowa, December 1980.

Blakely, M. "Why Would She Want To?" *Working Woman,* April 1985.

Bland, J. ed. *1984-85 Yearbook of Nutritional Medicine.* New Canaan,
Connecticut: Keats Publishing, 1985.

Bland, J. ed. *Nutraerobics,* San Francisco, California: Harper & Row, 1983.

Blumstien, P. *American Couples,* New York: William Morrow Company,
1983.

Brothers, J. *What Every Woman Should Know About Men.* New York: Simon
& Schuster, 1981.

Bruskin, R. H. "Lousy Women Drivers," *Glamour,* December 1985.

Caplan, B. "Crazy by Definition," *Savvy,* September 1986.

Cash, T. and Janda, L. "The Eye of the Beholder," *Psychology Today,*
December 1984. (References work by Kay Deaux and Laurie Lewis,
Purdue psychologists.)

Cash, T., Winstead, B., and Janda, L. "The Great American Shape-Up,"
Psychology Today, April 1986.

Cool, L. and Plummer, S. "Genetic Counseling," *Cosmopolitan,* June 1986.

de Simone, D. "You're No Weak Sister, Sister," *Mademoiselle,* May 1986.

177

Diagram Group, *Man's Body: An Owner's Manual,* New York: Bantam Books, 1976.

Donahue, P. *The Human Animal,* New York: Simon & Schuster, 1985.

Durden-Smith, J. and de Simone, D. *Sex and the Brain,* New York: Warner Books, 1983.

Edwards B. *Drawing on the Right Side of the Brain.* J.P. Tarcher, Inc., Los Angeles, California, 1979.

Garmon, L. "Of Hemispheres, Handedness and More." *Psychology Today,* November 1985. (About the late N. Geschwind.)

Elsea, J. *The Four-Minute Sell.* New York: Simon & Schuster, 1983.

Goleman, D. "Subtle But Intriging Differences Found In the Brain Anatomy of Men and Women," *New York Times,* Science Times, April 1989.

Goodman, D. Research presented to the Annual Meeting of the Society of Neuroscience, 1984.

Gould, R. *Men in the 80's: Old Questions, New Answers,* New York: Brunner/Mazel, 1985.

Gould, R. "Why Can't a (Working) Woman Be More Like a Man?" *Working Woman,* April 1985.

Grant, P. "Women, Work and Love." *Glamour,* July 1986.

Gwinup, G. "Man Scan." *Self,* April 1986. (Dr. Gwinup is Chairman of the Endocrinology and Metabolism Division at the University of California, Irvine School of Medicine.)

Hall, E. and Reinisch, J. "New Directions for the Kinsey Institute," *Psychology Today,* June 1986.

Harragan, B. "Getting Ahead - Management Training for Women," *Working Woman,* February 1984.

Hite, S. *Women and Love.* New York: Knopf, 1987.

Holzman, D. "Getting on Right Side of the Brain." *Insight,* October 1986. (About N. Geschwind's work.)

Horn, J. "Men, Women & Computer: Interest Matters," *Psychology Today,* July 1985. (A report about C.A.L.I.P. testing.)

Jeffcoate, W. *Journal of American Medical Association.* Psychosomatic Research, July 1988.

Kagan, J. "Survey - Work in the 1980's and 1990's," *Working Woman,* May 1983.

Keeton, K. *Woman of Tomorrow,* New York: St. Martins/Marek, 1985.

Kelves, B. "Nutritional Stress Studies," *Los Angeles Times,* May 1984. References Elsie M. Widdowson.

Kessler, R. and McRae, Jr., J. *American Sociological Review.* Study conducted 1976 at University of Michigan Institute for Social Research, 1982.

Kimura, D. "Male Brain, Female Brain: The Hidden Difference," *Psychology Today,* November 1985. (Kimura is a professor of psychology at Western Ontario University Hospital.)

Kolb, B. and Whishaw, I. *Fundamentals of Human Neuropsychology,* New York: W.H.Freeman and Co, 1980. (References "Thomas Water Level Task Report," University of Lethbridge.)

Landau, B. *Essential Human Anatomy and Physiology,* Second Edition. Dallas, Texas: Scott, Foresman and Company, 1980.

Lark, S. *Premenstrual Syndrome Self-Help Book,* Los Angeles, California: Forma Publishing, 1984.

Maccoby, E. and Jacklin, C. *The Psychology of Sex Differences,* Stanford, Connecticut: Stanford University Press, 1974.

Machlowitz, M. "MBA Management/Business Advice," *Working Woman,* September 1983.

Madaras, L. and Patterson, J. *Womancare,* New York: Avon Books, 1981.

Major, B. and Forcey, B. "Comparable Worth," *Journal of Experimental Social Psychology,* (Vol. 21, No. 4).

McGuinness, D. *When Children Don't Learn: Understanding the Biology and Psychology of Learning Disabilities,* New York: Basic Books, 1986.

McLoughlin, M. "Men vs. Women." *U. S. News & World Report,* August 1988. (References Ruben Gur's research.)

Mosedale, L. "Women Right Now," *Glamour,* December 1985.

Myers, D. *Social Psychology,* Hope College, Holland, Michigan: McGraw-Hill Books, 1983.

Paley V. *Boys and Girls: Superheroes in the Doll Corner,* Chicago, Illinois: University of Chicago Press, 1984.

Parrish, C. "Job Advice for Women," *Reader,* January 1984.

Rubin, Z. "Are Working Wives Hazardous to Their Husbands' Mental Health?" *Psychology Today,* May 1983.

Rubinstein, C. "How Men and Women Love," *Glamour,* April 1986.

Ruyle, S. "Women's Minds - The Current Flows Both Ways," *Dawn*, May 1986.

Sadker, M. and Sadker, D. "Sexism in the Schoolroom of the 80's." *Psychology Today*, March 1985.

Sandmaier, M. "When a Woman Smiles, Nobody Listens." *Mademoiselle*, July 1986.

Serlen, B. "Mutterings from the Men's Room," *Working Woman*, May 1983.

Sherman, M. and Haas, A. "Man to Man, Woman to Woman," *Psychology Today*, June 1984. (Based on research by professors of education at American University, Washington, D.C.)

Singer & Singer *Psychological Development in Children*. Philadelphia, Pennsylvania: W. B. Saunder, 1969.

Siwolop, S. "Why Women Get Cold." *Savvy*, June 1985.

Specter, M. "Coronary Bypass Surgery: Doctors Overlooking Women, New Study Says." *Los Angeles Times*, November 1987.

Staff Writer "Biological Factors May Tell the Boys from the Girls in Mathematics Tests," *Los Angeles Times*, Science/Medicine, June 1986. (Taken from research by Dr. Camilla P. Benbow, Iowa State psychologist.)

Staff Writer "Hormone that Cuts Heart Disease in Men Seems to Increase Risk in Women." *Los Angeles Times*, September 13, 1987. (Taken from research headed by Dr. Elizabeth Barrett-Conner, University of California, San Diego Dept.)

Staff Writer "In Sniffing Contests, Researchers Would Place Their Bets on Women." *Los Angeles Times*, Science/Medicine, June 1986. References R. Henkin, a Director of the Center for Molecular Nutrition & Sensory Disorders at Georgetown University.

Staff Writer "Virginia Slims American Women's Opinion Poll." *Family Circle*, February 1986.

Staff Writer "Women Have Own Business Style Says Poll," *Barnstormer*, July 1986. (Report on poll by California Business Magazine.)

Stechert, K. *Sweet Success: How to Understand the Men in Your Business Life and Win With Your Own Rules*. New York: Macmillan, 1986.

Steelman , L. and Powell, B. *Journal of Marriage and Family* (Vol. 47, No. 1), June 1985. (Steelman & Powell are sociologists at University of Southern Carolina and Indiana University, respectively.)

Switzer, E. "PMS, the Return of Raging Hormones," *Working Woman*, October 1983. (References research by Katharina Dalton.)

Symons, D. *The Evolution of Human Sexuality,* Oxford University Press, 1979. (Professor of anthroplogy at University of California, Santa Barbara, California.)

Taber's Cyclopedic Medical Dictionary, 13th Edition. F.A. Davis Company, 1977. (Reference for Klinefelter's Syndrome.)

The Sexual Brain. Video. Films for the Humanities, Inc., 1987.

Thompson, J. "Larger than Life." (Many women see themselves as round faced and pudgy even when no one else does.) *Psychology Today,* April 1986.

Trotter, R. "Mathematics: A Male Advantage?" *Psychology Today,* January 1987.

Wagenvoord, J. and Bailey, P. *Women: A Book for Men.* New York: Avon Books, 1979.

Walton, S. "The Second International Science Study." *Psychology Today,* June 1985, Texas A&M University. (Measured students' knowledge in grades 5, 9 and 12.)

Witelson, S. *Science* (Vol. 229, No. 4714). McMaster University, Hamilton, Ontario, 1982.

Wood, C. "Hormone Dominance." *Psychology Today,* October 1986.

Wood, C. "Masculinity and Mental Health," *Psychology Today.* (About S. Bem, a psychoogy at Stanford University.)

Wood W. *Journal of Personality and Social Psychology.* Vol. 48, No. 1.

INDEX